Praise for *Acquittal* for Mankind

"This is truly a fascinating read. Start reading today and be ready to be amazed, enlightened, awe-struck and inspired with these "unusual conversations". There isn't another book like it and you may find that these words are speaking directly to you."

– Peggy McColl
   New York Times Best-Selling Author

"Wolfgang Racher is not only a global expert in his field of healing; he is the best there is in engaging the spiritual side of your personality to help you create permanent change in your life through Theta Healing.

This book is a MUST for the serious student looking to understand and apply the ancient, yet little known and practiced universal principles of energy healing.

You are on the verge of a breakthrough, and with Wolfgang and this material, your best life is a guarantee – and that is no illusion!"

– Anders Hansen
   Illusionist, Keynote performer and change-maker

"This is an incredible book, written by "The Star Children" and brought to life by the incredible Wolfgang Racher.

This statement, from the intro of the book, represents the essence of this unique book *"This book, valued reader, is an invitation to your Soul to look at yourself and your life from the point of view of Love. It is precisely this that is sometimes so hard for us human beings to do."* It is only hard if we believe it to be. Wolfgang and friends will show you the way to view life with love, coming from your heart in all you do."

– Judy O'Beirn
   International Bestselling Author

Wolfgang Racher : Ishvara Elohim

Acquittal
for Mankind

Published by
Hasmark Publishing
www.hasmarkpublishing.com

First Edition printed in April 2007
© 2007 Ishvara Elohim

Second Edition as an ebook October 2017
© 2017 Wolfgang Racher—Ishvara Elohim

Third Edition paperback in October 2019
© 2019 Wolfgang Racher—Ishvara Elohim

All rights reserved. No part of this book, including excerpts, may be reproduced or transmitted in any form or by any means, electronic or mechanical, including photocopying, recording or by any information storage and retrieval system, without written permission from the author, except for the inclusion of brief quotations in a review.

Disclaimer

This book is designed to provide information and motivation to our readers. It is sold with the understanding that the publisher is not engaged to render any type of psychological, legal, or any other kind of professional advice. The content of each article is the sole expression and opinion of its author, and not necessarily that of the publisher. No warranties or guarantees are expressed or implied by the publisher's choice to include any of the content in this volume. Neither the publisher nor the individual author(s) shall be liable for any physical, medical, psychological, emotional, financial, or commercial damages, including, but not limited to, special, incidental, consequential or other damages. Our views and rights are the same: You are responsible for your own choices, actions, and results.

Permission should be addressed in writing to the author at freispruch@outlook.com

Translation from *Freispruch für die Menschheit* from the German edition by Christine Clover

Editor: Deborah Jones www.blueorchard.ca

Painting on the front cover by Silvian Sternhagel, Berlin www.licht-welten.com

Cover design: Angela Fürschuss, www.medienoffice.at

Layout: Anne Karklins
annekarklins@hasmarkpublishing.com

ISBN 13: 978-1-989161-99-9
ISBN 10: 1989161995

TABLE OF CONTENTS

Acknowledgements	8
Introduction	9
Greeting	13
Theater	19
Unhappiness	25
Forgiving—Pardoning	29
Memory—Love	31
Ambassador	35
Speech—Auto Repair Shop	37
Divine Will—Kingdom	41
The Beauty of Human Beings	43
A Blaze of Colour—Eyes of the Soul	47
Wisdom	51
Sound	55
It Is Possible!	59
Standing Still or Moving Forward?	63
Painting Class	67
A Secret	71
Elohim	75
Hate	79
Letting Go—Emotion	83
Inner Direction—Inner Godliness	87

The Source	91
Health	95
Evolutionary Step	99
Time	103
Polarity—Love	107
A Walk	111
Self-Esteem—Consciousness—Love	115
Inner Space	119
Spark	123
Power Station	127
Self-Love	129
Contrasts	133
Divine Motivation	137
God—Multiplicity	141
Treasure Chest	145
Appeal	149
Portrait of the Author	153

Acquittal for Mankind

Wolfgang Racher : Ishvara Elohim

How would you like to live your life without feelings of guilt? In this book the "Star Children-Elohim" speak of the light-filled nature of our cosmic origins. They describe an unusual view of mankind from a non-human, unconditionally loving perspective. Themes such as emotions, the search for meaning, spirituality, time, and health, seen from the polarizing view of human beings, are reduced to the common denominator of Love. Every reader can feel addressed personally and be motivated by a humorous and love-filled energy to live self-love as a basic human right.

This book can be understood as a loving guide in a time that is becoming ever faster…

Acknowledgements

I would like to thank the Star Children for their indescribably loving companionship!

My gratitude goes out to all companions on the path who remember their loving soul and spiritual origins and to all others as well who are living a life as Star Children without knowing it.

A very loving thanks above all to my family! In particular I would like to thank my mother, who knows how to share her light in such a joyous way. This book reminds us all of the blissful lightness of heart that children experience. For this reason I am grateful that my niece Hannah has joined our family.

My gratitude to everyone who through love, joy, and humor keep all of us cheerful. Thanks to all my companions!

Introduction

To the third edition from 2019

Dear Readers!

In the autumn of 2005 I felt myself being caressed by a wonderful, warm energy. To be sure, it took a few days until I turned my attention to this apparently new energy. The more I opened myself up to this loving presence, the clearer it became. Finally, voices from within this pleasant sensation became audible, loudly and clearly. I had scarcely found the courage to listen to these voices when I was given the invitation in an unbelievable bath of love to trust these beings, which all spoke as one voice. Thus the first chapter of this book was born, without my knowing it. Only in the course of further "conversations" did it become clear to me that my counterparts, who introduced themselves to me as the "Star Children," were asking me to publish a book about them. Looking back, this is funny, as I had been carrying the title of a book around in my head without in any way intending to really write a book. I just thought that if I ever did write a book it would have to have the title "Acquittal for Mankind." We can see here once again in a splendid way just how carefully the spiritual world works within the synchronicity of time itself. Time seems to play quite a different role from what we human beings would often like it to.

This book has no foreword in the usual sense as the Star Children themselves have written a wonderful introduction with the first chapter of greeting. My concern here is merely to present a short introduction to the unusual view of mankind with which this book concerns itself.

This book, valued reader, is an invitation to your Soul to look at yourself and your life from the point of view of Love. It is precisely this that is sometimes so hard for us human beings to do. Often, something that catches our interest is then dismissed in a superficial manner because we make a judgement about it and categorize it as being either good or bad. This book remains consistent in regarding mankind from a non-human, absolutely loving perspective. The Star Children describe where the Spirit and the Soul of human beings actually come from, what their true nature is, and for what purpose they incarnate here on the Earth. With the same loving quality they also describe the great upheavals that are taking place at this time on our planet and in the solar system; in this regard, one should turn one's attention to one's self, as it is there that these upheavals are to be found! On the other hand, however, any reader who is looking here for prophesies of doom will be disappointed. Fear can never bring about a transformation to a higher level of consciousness!

Due to the different quality of time within spiritual dimensions you can feel yourself spoken to personally at any time by what you read here! One can feel this particularly when reading the introductory words to each chapter. The Star Children have made it clear to me that they are speaking personally to every reader in their messages! In that way, if you are a female reader, you will find it easier to overlook the occasional use of masculine forms of address. As I have noticed in myself, and the Star Children have also reassured me: while reading, Soul and Spiritual energies are activated and in that way processes of Spiritual healing are set in motion. In this way, it will become easier and faster to dissolve into the Love-filled energy of one's own Spirit. Thus, when one reads a chapter a number of times it can happen that its content reveals itself to you from a wholly new perspective. What is changing is not the texts themselves—what is changing is you!

In a number of the texts I have allowed myself to add a word in brackets […] that I consider important to a better understanding of a sentence.

Comments on the 3rd edition:

This book is concerned exclusively with the point of view of the Star Children toward mankind, not with human ways of looking at things, and not with my own, for that matter. Nevertheless I would like to point something out, in brief: there is, as in all other forms of communication, here as well naturally a sender and a receiver. Every receiver is in a certain sense a filter which has been formed by all conscious, and above all unconscious, experiences in life. In direct communication with the Star Children it did not surprise me all that much that a part of my conscious mind was shut down during our communications—I had been familiar with this state of mind for a good while—but rather that a new, unfamiliar, and limitless space opened itself up to me. In this space I found no foothold, no matter how much I tried to orient myself or hold on to things—there was space and only space! This communication was always a venture that took place solely within my heart. Only in that way could I listen freely to the inspiration, without bringing myself into it. It was strange, but whenever I noticed that a topic concerned me directly, shortly afterward the fear arose in me that the Star Children would let the whole world know something very personal about my own life. It took willpower to remain absolutely trusting! In the end, while listening, I found myself in an indescribable bath of Love, and once again in a limitless space.

I am relating this as there is a single chapter in the book that came about in quite a different way. I was uncertain for a long time about what I should do with it, as even today this text is as far as I can determine different from all the others in its energy. It elicits a different reaction in me compared to all the other texts. But maybe I am the only one who feels this way? At first I thought that the chapter "Theater" would have no place in the book, as it came about in a totally different way: although, here, I was also awoken by my dear friends in the middle of the night, as with every other chapter, yet I was to find myself only at the beginning and at the end of this "conversation" in that limitless space.

With "Theater" I was in the midst of the story, I experienced it, I lived it, I understood it, I **was** this story. And thus, dear readers, this chapter is even today a very special didactic piece of theater, and perhaps those who read this chapter "Theater" understand it better and more readily than I do.

Full of joy, I hope that this book poses questions that find their answers in your heart and your Soul! The Divine Presence of the Star Children,

"ELOHIM", can give you a little taste of where you come from and where you will go after your earthly journey.

The key to these messages is Love!

How good that this book has found its way to you!

    Wolfgang Racher : Ishvara Elohim

Greeting

Finally, at long last, you are here! At last you are all here! This is the point in time, the moment that we have waited for, for a long time. We were being prepared for this moment, you and we, for a long time. We are meeting here according to an old agreement—according to an agreement that still stands. Yes, that is how it is.

A beautiful light is visible, surrounding your heart. It resembles more and more who we are, and who you truly are. Our meeting in the NOW is a great joy. Now you allow us and you to come close to one another. This is a true honor for all of us. This does not mean that we are not close to each other otherwise. It means that HERE and NOW, [in your consciousness], you have given permission for it. While we are speaking to you, you are opening yourself up more and more to your true nature. This is something old and familiar, at this meeting, even if it appears as something new to you in this form.

"Who are you?" you will ask. We are beings from the starry heavens. We are a kind of task force that has been ordered here to help you with your work. Our work is solely **LOVE**. Your work is solely **LOVE**, nothing else. Now you may perhaps object: "Oh, really? I'm in the thick of it here, in this life, and you say that my only work is Love." Yes! Your work is Love. And so that you are able to accept yourself, more and more, we will help you to view your earthly constraints, such as self-condemnation, depression, and addiction to power, from another perspective, as all of this has served throughout the eons to make it possible to live within these earthly constraints on the Earth. You have now come in order to overcome them. This great Love is YOU. You are equipped with everything you need here. So take heart, and do not worry. You have all the tools that you need in order to do your work here with joy.

We came here in a kind of space ship. That may well sound odd to you, even if it is increasingly likely to find a place in the world of your imagination. You could also imagine it like this: we move from celestial body to celestial body with our consciousness. We connect to the place we are traveling to with our consciousness. And that is also your true nature, Beloved Creature. You too move with your consciousness throughout the various planes of existence. A marvelous space ship! It takes you everywhere you are able to imagine it doing so. **Thus, your consciousness serves you as a means of locomotion!** Consciousness, as you experience it, has various—let us call it—levels of speed. Those are the speeds of your space ship—from a slow, ambling tempo to the ability to be everywhere at once. Isn't that an unbelievable bandwidth of locomotion opportunities?

These speeds are different forms of your orientation. They are also dependent on your identification with the landscape as it passes by. Thus, the particular path you have chosen to take is your own locomotion speed. If you are in conflict with something, your space ship stands still, or moves only very, very slowly. Those are situations in which you think you will apparently never overcome the obstacle. The other extreme would be that you feel yourself to be AT ONE with your destination. Then there is no distance, no separation any more between you and your destination. Then you have achieved a moment of becoming one with your destination—it can go that fast! Here on the Earth, when you are moving through your landscape, you always choose the right speed for yourself in which you see the things as you want to see them, until you see them as they ARE. And that is a huge challenge that you have taken upon yourselves here. We congratulate you on this! Even if this may still sound confusing to you, you will understand more and more why your work here is so prized, why you are loved so very much. It is because you have voluntarily put on a much narrower, smaller and more uncomfortable garment over your radiant, shining robe of light. For that reason you can't recognize the light that you truly are, so readily. That is the reason why you are esteemed.

We are not the only ones who bring you this message. Whenever cosmic beings meet in Love on this planet, they bring towards you this same deep respect, this esteem, this Love, because of your service here. Now the time for our meeting is ripe, and that is very good!

Good, as we already mentioned, we are here to assist you in recognizing this monstrosity, this great boulder, this powerful ILLUSION of the earthly for what it is. We want to show you possibilities, in Love, and support you in moving forward, in order to decipher the obstacles as well as the illusions, to see them for what they are. With deciphering we mean this: we will give you a "**special pair of glasses**." When you use them, you will say "Oh, that's how it is! Oh, that is what is meant! But everything makes sense now! If I had known that earlier, I would not have allowed myself to be put off so often by the outward effects of those obstacles!" These glasses will reveal the blueprint for your life's journey to you and replace your fear and worry with joy.

It is the case, however, that you have come to Earth, and meet your world here from a restricted point of view. But by recognizing its true nature—WHAT IT IS—you are acting less for yourself personally and are more a part of the Great Plan, the great development. You are one of many who have decided to do service here in the same way. That is what you have all come for. Since we have come in Love, it will become more and more enlightening and uplifting for you to accept our assistance, if you wish to do so.

We have waited for you here on this plane of vibration until you have allowed the form of consciousness that permits us to speak the same language. But we would also like to tell you that the great Love found in the Divine Source is in EVERYTHING. No matter how dense the spheres seem to be through which you pass—God's Love is everywhere! Everything you encounter is a part of God. Love is present on all planes and dimensions. We tell you this, so that you can recognize that spiritual development goes hand-in-hand with Love.

There is no spiritual progress for you human beings without Love. If you believe yourselves to be very far advanced in general because you make use of this or that **technology** in order to set yourselves above the rest of your own kind, you will discover that the search for security and support within this always creates a further dependency, namely one on spiritual Love—spiritual Love is the key!

Assistants are available on all planes who help respective beings to gain experience. We are meeting here on this plane of perception and know how beautiful and loving you are experiencing them to be. It is easy for us to always move about in this radiant robe of light. For you, with an earthly consciousness, it has meant a great deal of effort to be here where you now are. With that, we come to speak of your reincarnation. It is your divine work. It is no penal colony, to which you are sent again and again to do penance, even if you have seen it like that for a long time, as this view helped you to suppress yourselves so that you might wear the dark robe for as long as possible. At times this view also helped you to do your work here and to justify it. Now, however, it is high time to refrain from this kind of work. You have gone through many trials. If this "old" point of view still appeals to your earthly consciousness, then look at it like this:

Now you have earned the right to wear the robe of light again!

We are with you in great Love. In this way we want to show you that we and you exist on the same plane, but in different forms of expression. We will continue to help you with your work. If you wish, you can look at it like this: **you have been given a new position**. Your old employment contract was amicably terminated. You received good compensation for it, and now you are taking up a new position—welcome to your first day of work! Of course it is not your very first day of work, but doesn't it feel somewhat like it? Isn't a good feeling? Congratulations on your new position, on your new profession, on your new job!

We will always keep a notepad handy that you can glance at whenever you want to know what is next on the schedule for you to do. Yes, that sounds very good—our service is in that way very well described. We are here and working together with you in your new position. We have high hopes of good and collegial work and cooperation with one another, and as well, that we enjoy our time together. We now invite you to have a bit of a look around your new work place and take a look at your new rooms. Have a look out the window to see just where it is you have landed now. We are certain you will like it! As you see, you are not alone. There are a good number working in this special company. There are also very many who keep on applying to work here. Or those who have already been offered the job, but who did not turn up for their first day at work. Even that is completely all right.

Here there is no condemnation such as you are familiar with! We are going to show you around a little and show you other rooms. We will introduce you to your new place of work and show you what tasks you have taken on here, what fields of activity, so to speak, fall within your competence.

And we will continue this form of communication in Love, whenever you are ready for it—Beloved. We will become more and more of a reality for you.

You are loved, and all of you are loved!

    The Star Children

Theater

We greet you with a bath of light full of Love! How good that you are here again. It is good that you are still interested in further instructions for your new profession. We would like to show you something.

To that end, imagine, please, the following: you are in a very beautiful theater and sitting in the audience. You have the best seat in the house and from this position you are watching everything that is happening on the stage. You are following very closely the course of the play that is now being performed. You are watching the characters and the story. Soon you are so impressed by this play and its dramatic developments that it casts more and more of a spell over you, until you feel **as though you were right in the middle of the events on the stage**. You experience the characters, the plot, and all the emotions that the actors are portraying here as closely as possible. Suddenly, all that which is being performed turns into life itself, into your own life. You are in the role of the actor! Suddenly you recognize yourself in this play in the midst of your own everyday life again, in the midst of situations that you already recognize. Everything is so real. All the actors you meet are somehow suddenly no longer actors but rather **are** in their full range of feeling what they are portraying. The scenery weaves itself completely into the story no matter which props are used next to you in the play. It doesn't matter if a scene takes place in the city, in the country, or in any other place, you are all of a sudden entirely caught up in the events. You perceive everything as clearly as though it were being played just for you. You play your own role in the meantime so well that you know: everything that is happening here is reality.

Now you find yourself in a situation in which contrasting opinions confront one another. Because you play your role so authentically, with all its emotions, you know that YOUR perception of the events is the right one. All the emotions that you experience seem to you to be entirely justified. For that reason, at times you feel treated unfairly due to the unexpected reaction of the other actors.

Let's say that the plot of the play develops in such a way that from one side of the stage an actor comes towards you and takes you to task. Now you could say: "Why do I have to listen to that? Do I really have to put up with it?" With that, other feelings are called forth in you, perhaps feelings of resentment? And without thinking about it, it becomes clear to you that you are entitled to react in that way. You respond to your counterpart in an aggressive manner and are already in the midst of the play. A very normal situation in everyday life could happen like this, couldn't it?

But, honored members of the audience, let us remember how this story actually began. You were seated in the audience, and watched how this whole play turned into reality. Just now you were still caught up in your role and said and did what this role demanded of you. You reacted the way you had always reacted, and gave it your best shot.

Suddenly, however, you see yourself from the outside. What you saw on the stage and just now performed in such a real way, you now view as "acting." You are still sitting in the best seat in the house and attending this play as an observer. Of course, when the emotions and the plot move you, it is possible to become once again part of the play. Now, however, you can recognize that in that case you are taking on the role of the actor, although you are sitting in the audience.

So far, so good! Now we want to show you a possibility or remind you of a possibility that you are already familiar with. Now, however, we want to make it attractive to you in a particular way. What you can do now, from your seat in the audience, is not merely to observe but, in a different and perhaps new way, to intervene in the play and thus, to shape the play.

A familiar scene plays out on the stage once again. The actor in this scene is once again accused of something by another and taken to task.

You see this from the audience. Now the scene begins to get even more heated and it increases in intensity. Yet before you slip into the role of the actor as you believe you understand the situation and consider the way he is defending himself to be justified, you now have the opportunity to become active in your new role as director of the play.

In this moment you can say **STOP**.

For a moment, in peace, look at what other possibilities there are available to this actor to react instead of plunging emotionally into a fight. It might also be that at the moment there is still a great deal within you that resists taking advantage of this new activity as the action in the scene has been familiar to you for a long time, and you considered the reaction to be justified. Perhaps you sense, for once, how it feels from the point of view of the audience to watch the play and at the same time to be happy that you are not personally involved in the play. Yes, personally! Perhaps this distance from the role of the actor is so pleasant for you that you say, "My God, am I happy that this is not my life and that the part he is playing is not my fate!" To say STOP means that for a short moment at least you find it attractive not to be the actor and not to be associated with the suffering in this role.

You can now give the actor directions as to how he should behave in this situation. It is much easier, from your distance in your seat in the audience, not to get caught up in the emotions that are being played out on the stage. For that reason, out of your rich store of experience you now give this actor a possibility to play the part in a different way. Think about it: someone has taken him furiously to task—that was the part. It was very, very well thought-out. This scene was very meticulously developed and wrapped in a story line without the actor being aware of anything until it came to this "attack." For the audience, who was astounded by all this, the length of this scene almost seemed to constitute a play in itself. This scene played out for the audience in a different dimension in time than for the actor. Now make use of this other temporal dimension to intervene in the manner of response to the part without the audience noticing it. Our intention is to help the actor not to feel offended, so that he can deal with his role more easily. Don't worry—the play won't become any less exciting; it will become at least just as exciting. So you can go ahead and "rewrite" the part and change it.

Good, the action is still suspended, so what do you tell the actor now? What instructions do you give him? You need to consider in addition that he is so convinced by his part that you have to tell him clearly how he is to react so as to dissuade him from his normal manner of reacting. We are therefore asking you for clear directions. The simplest direction might be that the actor shouldn't react in the same way as before. Further instructions could be that he should now show traits of character which an older and wiser person possesses who has gone through a great deal in his life, and for whom that which he is being accused of here no longer affects him personally. Because of his many experiences and adventures in life he knows how to assess something like this and knows just how "seriously" he should take it. Now tell the actor that he should play the role in this way!

The scene on stage begins. The second actor begins once again to scream at him in fury and to launch accusations at him. Watch the reactions of your actor very closely now, and see how calmly he accepts it all, how little he seems to be affected by it emotionally, indeed, with what insight he listens to the screaming of the man standing across from him. Isn't it at least just as interesting for the audience as it was before? Was the audience expecting such a reaction? We think that it is even very good to rewrite the part and change it in this way. The second actor can hardly believe the reaction that he is getting from your actor. He begins to repeat the scene; he loses his temper once again and begins to berate our figure in the worst way. Because our actor is now playing the part of the insightful, wise, old man, he understands his counterpart's motivation that drives him to such emotions. He himself has also reacted in such a manner when he felt himself to be misunderstood. Thus it doesn't affect him personally any more. The second actor is aghast, and asks himself if he is perhaps not playing his part convincingly enough? Perhaps he will repeat his scene again for a third time. Your actor will once again react with the same insight as before.

"Wait a minute!" the audience will now say. "It's starting to get a little boring here. Is this a director's error, or an error in the plot, in the script, in the original novel, in the original source material?" as now the rest of the audience is also picking up on the difference between the new and old ways of playing the two scenes, and in this way a new identification and sympathy with your actor's new way of playing the part has been aroused in a number of them. Perhaps interest for the new scene has been aroused even in those who still might have reacted in the old way. That's how easy it is to rewrite a play.

Now we'll let the second actor decide for himself how he will continue with his part. Perhaps it even feels odd to him if he insists on playing his old role again, or perhaps he alters his role as well. We are certain that if he continues his part in the way he has up to now, he will garner no sympathy from the side of the audience. The spectators would chase him from the stage, as it is getting to be a bore. He can decide, at this point, to leave or to play his part in a different way. Great relief on the part of the audience! The play being performed still retains its very gripping content. It deals with the same topics. The plot was only rewritten to the extent that the actors were given additional opportunities to react to the dialogue. The second actor now has the opportunity to present the words that he has to speak in a different way; **to present what he really has to say in a new manner**. If he were still caught up in the old emotions, as an actor, and wouldn't have wanted to change, he would have had to look for another theater company! He plays his part differently—so that it is appropriate to the reaction of the other actor. The content has taken on another meaning through the new way of playing the parts.

We congratulate you on your role as theater director. You solved the problem in a fascinating way. The actors can keep on acting and keeping the audience amused and affected. You now know: you have the possibility at any time to have your actors play their parts the way you would like them to. Earlier, you often forgot your position as observer, as you were so fascinated by what was being played. You were right in the midst of the role. Now you know once more that you are a spectator and at the same time, by means of this wonderful kind of theater, that you have the possibility of shaping the scene the way you would like it to be.

We now invite you to take a scene out of your life and to have it played out on the stage, perhaps initially as you remember it and then changing the scene for so long until you as a spectator are really convinced by the way it is performed. In the end, that is what theater is for. What do you think of it all? Keep intervening in the part, whenever you feel like it, until you really like the play. We will let you be the director, and wish you a lot of fun in your new role.

We spoke of a new job for you. This is it. You have been promoted to theater director. Think about it: the play should be gratifying to everyone! And—the part you play on the stage **is your own part—it is your life**. It's all theater!

We wish you a lot of enjoyment in your work. We see that there are a lot of new actors on the stage and that in this new, modern theater you are making use of all the possibilities to dramatize your life. Perhaps it will even occur to you to have angels play roles as well—giving angels a part? It's all theater! What would be wrong with that? It's all theater!

Have fun building your sets, organizing your props, handing out the parts!

We will meet again with you the next time—in Love!

    Your Friends from the Stars

Unhappiness

Hello, Beloved, Precious One, Beloved, Precious One, Beloved, Precious One!

So you are unhappy? Then we want to speak with you about unhappiness. What is unhappiness? Unhappiness is a form of cleansing, of letting go. Unhappiness is a special quality that exists together with you in your density.

We would like to remind you that you are a multi-dimensional being, which is capable of experiencing feelings within a great bandwidth and nevertheless at the same time to exist within Love. Whenever you are within a feeling, we see you in this energy and at the same time within the Love that you are. What you perceive in this condition is usually only the emotion. Thus, emotion is a condition, an aid, to perceiving a very particular aspect of your reality, as for example unhappiness.

Unhappiness is like a sluice. If you open it, you are opting for a cleansing process of this kind. We don't need to tell you what unhappiness feels like. You experience it for yourself. But we can speak to you about the background to unhappiness and want to remind you once again that Love is found in everything—also in unhappiness. To be unhappy is related to the pain of loss. That means that something wants to pass beyond your perception, and you have decided to hold on to it to consider it to be something **real**! But it can only move on if you don't hold it back. The more you try to hold on to it, the greater your unhappiness will be.

There are many different facets and degrees of unhappiness. It is an aspect of your earthly existence throughout your entire life, as life is constantly moving past you and you constantly have to decide whether you will allow it to, or whether you will cling to it. Thus, unhappiness is an emotion that is very strongly connected to being human. For that reason we invite you not to judge yourself for your unhappiness. If you allow unhappiness to be what it is, namely a tool of Love, then you give it the opportunity to be a tool of transformation. Unhappiness is always a mirror that reflects the fact that in your earthly existence you feel subliminally to be separated from Divine Love. We have already spoken about this, as this is a means of expression of the powerful Maya—illusion—that was also given to you as a tool on your path.

If you want to transform unhappiness, then the most direct means that you have at your disposal is: **allowing it to be!** Allow that to be, what is. This will calm your thoughts, assuage your worries, and give your Love the opportunity to unfold. Allowing it to be also means to recognize it. Allowing it to be is in this case the most powerful thing you can do, as then you release the **energy of transformation within the tool of unhappiness** and use it so that it is integrated into your life as a natural element in it.

Do not be hard on yourself because of your unhappiness! It is evidence that you are being asked to move forward at a very fast pace! You will see where it is all headed only when you get moving! And as you move along, you will see that we are waiting for you at your destination.

We would like to congratulate you human beings! We would like to congratulate you on successfully coping with your dense, many-sided world of emotional experience! We would like to continue this conversation as we began it and remind you that unhappiness generally represents an opportunity to deal with your earthly life—thus it is a form of transformation. Unhappiness is something that takes you from one experience to the next.

Imagine this as a circle. Place yourself at the center of the circle. The circumference is your world of experiences in the outer world, and unhappiness is one of the many means of locomotion along the line of this circle which you follow in your life. If you stand in the middle and observe this, you will see how many possibilities there are to move forward, until you have traveled the entire circumference of the circle and have arrived back to where you started. If you stand in the middle, you then see that unhappiness is one of the many modes of the expression of Love. It is permitted to draw you closer to your goal, if you accept unhappiness as such. In that case, then, it is not merely self-serving, and then you are no longer held prisoner in this emotion.

You are blessed in your world of experiences. We also call it an adventure park, your amusement park. Perhaps you are now finding it easier to sense that unhappiness is one form of experience. It is a form of expression in the theater that you visit in your amusement park, and as you know that there is so much more to experience, it is also easier for you to find the exit to the theater.

Think about it! Our Love is your Love, your Love is our Love. A part of you is always with us, and only a part of you is a visitor to this amusement park. The entry ticket that you have paid for allows you to look at all the attractions—it is valid for the entire adventure park!

We are the Star Children, and accompany you on your journey!

Forgiving — Pardoning

We greet you! It is so good to see your readiness to communicate with us.

We are here every time to express our Love to you, our Love that we have for you and for every Child of Man. We would like to tell you how important it is to forgive and to pardon. If you find yourselves in painful situations or in situations of negative emotions then the most positive and effective thing you can do is **to forgive**.

By forgiving you come to the heart of the matter. By forgiving you can come so close to the core of the emotion that it becomes even easier to accept it. Isn't that a nice plot twist? Thus, you move away from your fixed point of view towards a point of view where there is not only room for everything but also where you can recognize yourself as creator, as co-creator, of these situations. We have already spoken to you about this a number of times, but would like to emphasize once again the importance of this message.

Forgiveness is ONE way that leads to independence!

What is meant by independence? Autonomy! In these times in which you are now here, during which the vibrations on this planet are becoming finer, you are permitted to look behind the scenes in order to discover more about how earthly dramas work, and the possibilities of resolving them. Forgiveness is a key to these possibilities. So, whom can you forgive? You can forgive others for reflecting your own ideas and beliefs, for reflecting them and making them visible. Above all, however, you can forgive yourselves that you as creator also co-created such situations. Forgiving is a kind of **recognition** and of **letting go**.

Why do you tend to look for the fault outside of yourselves and in others? Because you have not yet learned to forgive yourselves!

To forgive one's self is the most important tool for anyone who wants to set off consciously on the path!

Forgive yourself, and the vibration becomes finer!

We love you!

    The Star Children

Memory — Love

We greet you, Beloved, Precious One!

It is so nice to be with you. You perceive us in a very particular way, in your way. **We are with you**, and this also includes your human presence. That means that we are with your entire being. It is so good to see you, to perceive you in your Love, your greatness, your devotion. You are our friend. You knew that long before we met each other, because our meeting became valid at that moment that you set off on your journey, your journey to the Earth.

"Er…for what purpose are you here again?" you might ask now. We are here, to remind you that you are a part of God which accepted the gift of entering into service in the "Here and Now." The service that you human beings do here is truly a great one. It is much more than you generally can perceive. Being here means being entirely committed. It also means here, within time, the time during which you have forgotten and are not able to see who you are, to actually relearn once again that it is also possible, even here, to exist more and more in Love.

The service that you do here, as we have already said, is something you are not only doing for yourselves, but also for others, for this planet, for the Being of Earth, for everyone.

Recently it seems as though confusion has played a prominent role within your development. You have come in order to make it possible for Love to exist by means of your personal existence, by your personal actions. The closer this Love comes, however, the more you also meet with confusion. "Are those not two contrasting qualities?" you might ask. Yes and no! Love was given to you so that you might also perceive it in confusion as well. You have met with confusion in order to see Love within it. For that reason we want to reassure you: it doesn't matter whether you perceive yourself to be on the path or standing still, no longer knowing what direction life should take…**you are always on your path**, no matter what it looks like to you!

Of course we can see this much easier from our side, as we are able to admire you as a whole. But if you once view this situation from our standpoint, by means of your imagination and fantasy—by means of your heart—and with the readiness to be able to see it and with the willingness to see it—you will also perceive it in this way. Taking up this position means to accept your path, to perceive it independently from and unconditioned by your human ideas, and to see it for what it is. That's it! Allowing your human concepts to vibrate more and more within the cosmic frequency of Divine Love—that is your path!

You are able to meet with many experiences, here on your journey, and to find yourselves once again in various meetings that are related to your memories—through the energy of recollection—that connect you to particular situations and emotions and draw you to them. Thus such situations attract you to them, and them to you, as the energy of recollection that is stored within the situation and also within you, is the **same** energy.

As you already know, Beloved Creature of God, Beloved Friend, the earthly capacity to remember is very much limited to what it has perceived **up to now. To connect this capacity of recall with Inspiration means a way out of such situations**. Now, that may sound to many of you a little confusing. For that reason we would like to explain it to you somewhat. The short version of the explanation is this:

You meet God in every situation.

What reason could there possibly be not to trust that everything in your life is as it should be? Perhaps this, that your ability to remember—this is your earthly consciousness here—can most easily identify with and warm to what it already knows on the earthly plane, that is, that which is already present in your memory. This can contain a multitude of experiences. There is room for every kind of emotion in it. Thus it would be good if you were able to keep the bigger picture in mind, in such situations, so that you might recognize that in painful meetings with others it was identification and memory that were the forces that attracted you to such situations.

And the way to release this is to allow another force into your existence, one that is always present. This is your **Divine Power of Perception**. It knows all and is all. It is not limited by that which you can remember here, or by that which you hold to be true here. Thus, if a situation seems to be hopeless, connect yourself to your Inspiration by means of your faith. Connect yourself by means of your heart with your Inspiration and it will show you a way of seeing beyond that which you now know. A part of your path consists of allowing space for Divine Power, Inspiration, and Intuition in all situations. This means elevating earthly vibration. The memory of emotions leads to identification, which also leads to a conflict with your true nature. This conflict only exists for the purpose of providing a space for your true nature, your true being, and your greatness at this moment. In this way, the memory becomes a Divine Memory.

Now of course you can say, "Good, that is easy enough to comprehend whenever I find myself within Love—for example, while I am reading this. But how should I do this when I appear to be caught up in an emotional situation, when I am struggling with my lot in life?" That is very easy: by knowing that you don't have to do anything in particular at all! Quite the opposite, in fact. The best thing for you to do is nothing at all, simply sit down, and for one—or more—or even quite a few moments, just BE. This means transformation. This dissolves the feeling of being imprisoned, of holding on, the apparent feeling of being stuck. Thus it is the opposite of the way you have changed situations up to now. We would like to offer this way, our way of seeing things, to you simply as a possibility. The only thing that you need in order to do this is a power that you already possess—this quality is a part of your nature: it is **SURRENDER**.

All around you there is a lot of joy, and the light of your Soul is visible. It is celebrating a festival of jubilation, because it has looked forward to, and has been waiting, waiting in faith for, our meeting with one another in the "Here and Now."

We love you, Divine Creature! We see who you truly are. We see your beauty, your greatness, and your devotion. Your experiences, your earthly experiences, everything that comes to meet you in your life, come from Love. There is only Love. We love you, we are with you!

We look forward to continuing this form of communication!

    Your friends, the Star Children

Ambassador

A most hearty good morning to our friends on the Earth! We are placing our words into your heart. Yes, they are set into your heart like letters.

We have come once more, to laugh with you, to celebrate, and to raise a toast with you to the joyful event that has taken place in the cosmic realm. Something has taken place that is contained in the plan of the "Great Entirety", something the times are ready for. Here on the Earth a further "evolutionary step" has taken place for, through, and with all of you. Those who remain entirely confident within their hearts and their spiritual truths are finding it particularly easy at this moment. They know that everything that is and will come takes place to the highest degree of perfection. Those who are still somewhat busy with the breakdown of their patterns of belief have chosen a somewhat more difficult path.

Breakdown, what is that? We have often spoken of the Light-Body Process. You have already heard a great deal regarding the Light-Body Process, the connection of your divine consciousness with your earthly consciousness. We call the continuous fusion of your earthly consciousness with your divine consciousness, breakdown. A nicer word for it would surely be "process of refinement." But even all that is to be regarded without evaluation and judgment, as everything that happens is totally fine!

You who are sailing along on the wave of Divine Faith, and you, who are still struggling and swimming against the tide of Love: **Let yourselves simply be drawn by, be attracted by, the power of God**. This is once again a call to think about all your activities and to review them in your hearts. In the moment that you do this, you are allowing yourselves to be drawn towards your destination by your own divinity. It can be that easy! All of this has already been said in various ways. We will continue to say it often to you in order to help you and to assist you so that you are able more and more often to settle into the divine wave of Love, of surrender, of trust, and of power. This is like a timetable that can help you to arrive at your destination with confidence. Isn't that wonderful? An awareness of the inner divine guidance has already progressed so far with so many of you that your so-called process of ascension is making great strides.

We ask you to see the divine mission in each and every one of you! Look at other people like this from within your hearts. That gives them and you an opportunity to fulfill their personal tasks within the greater plan. You are masters of many dimensions at the same time. That means you guide your human existence not only by means of your earthly consciousness. That is a part of your corporeal existence and is nourished by your senses, and for that reason you are esteemed, for that which you take upon yourselves.

You are the ambassadors of the Divine Light, the Divine Source—just as an ambassador is sent to another country to be a representative of his homeland. Of course, all countries are part of the whole, for example part of the Earth, part of a planet, part of a larger entity. This conversation should remind you that you are **ambassadors.** You have decided to come here as ambassadors and to represent the Source. Your service here was for a long time a secret mission "undercover." You have often led the life of a secret agent. Now it will become easier and easier to reveal your true identity and to show it openly.

We love you so much, our friends, who do your work on the Earth. You are the true masters. We can learn from you. Be honored, you representatives of the Divine Creation, the Divine Oneness, the Divine Existence. All who do service on, in, and around this planet Earth are doing their utmost so that your awakening might resemble a dawn. If you open your eyes and see the Divine Light in everything, this will resemble a clear dawn of day. Thus we are with you every day of your existence in Love, solidarity, and joy.

We greet you!

Your Star Children

Speech — Auto Repair Shop

We greet you, our beloved and valued friend. Be open, be empty.

We greet you, our beloved and valued friend. We are waiting for you and are always ready to get in touch with you. We are happy that you are here again.

Today we want to discuss **LANGUAGE** and talk about **SPEECH** with you.

Speech is something that you human beings have only made use of fairly recently in the course of your entire evolution. The language you use is unique. It is a part of your particular culture and expresses above all what moves you, causes you concern, and makes you happy. There are various languages. One of them is the **language of the heart**. Perhaps you have already noticed that in a condition of Love you use the language of the heart? That means: the more you allow yourselves to be guided by your inner voice, the more often you use the language of your heart; it doesn't need any human words. We would like to remind you that during the time you were establishing yourselves on this planet, you made do without human language. As the veil became denser, you could remember less and less of your home, your true nature. As this journey continued the language of the heart fell more and more silent. Thus human language developed, as even in this "darkness" forms of communication were necessary.

Among animals, and they are in a certain way related to you, language is still somewhat similar to the language of the heart than it sometimes is with you human beings. We as spiritual beings use a kind of telepathy as a means of communicating. This is the appropriate way for us to communicate, because compared to your human every-day consciousness we repose much more within BEING, KNOWLEDGE, and FAITH.

Whenever your hearts stop speaking you human beings use the verbal form of speech often as a substitute, rather than the language of heart; then you allow your words to speak, so to speak. But we are here to remind you how you can find the way into the heart, back to faith and to your true nature once again. And we would like to encourage you to use the language of the heart. We are saying this to you in the language of the heart. This helps you to communicate in an unambiguous way.

If one would like to share and give a portion of one's BEING, one can use the language of the heart. It is a very quick and direct way, which leads you to your true nature. The language of the heart does not need any words, any spoken words. The language of the heart uses the inner perceptions of BEING and communicates this in the same quality to the next person. We want to encourage you to use your human language and allow it to become the language of the heart. We want to remind you how it is when your every spoken word is used as a pathway to the heart. In this way you human beings really share a portion of what your true nature is. We would like to tell you that language can spread very intense energy and can bring out what is within you. You often use it to spread mental energy in your surroundings. It works in that case precisely according to the quality in which you use it. Language is a miracle drug: it can heal—it can kill!

Dear, valued friend, we have been waiting for you. We want to convey our joy at our relationship, the joy that you are our mouthpiece and allow language to flow out from your center of Love. Don't worry: every word is a means of expressing your heart. You are allowing the words, our words, to become your words again and pass them on in order to create inner peace. Love, peace and harmony, that's what you say, isn't it? We are with you so that you capture the energy in words, in language, in order to give people there, where they are at that moment, our Love and your Love. You are so full of Love that it is a real joy to be together with you within your light. Always follow your heart, follow Love—that is your path! It will always encourage you to keeping following it, remaining open for what the great source of joy holds ready for you. Through your openness and readiness, you become a part of your true nature. Through your Love, you are a part of your true nature.

We are with you in great Love. We assist you and help you not to judge yourself, but rather to accept yourself. We show you your own truth. We show you your truth and your inner nature until you recognize yourself as a vessel of Divine Love and perceive your nature as Divine Love. Your nature is great joy, devotion and Love. It is what drives you here on the Earth. It is the motivation that unites the Spirit, the Soul with your body. There is no other reason besides Love why you human beings do your service here. It is because of Love that you take everything upon yourselves, namely, living in darkness here. You are the ones who are helping the Earth in its process of advancement and bringing about the necessary transformation in order to make the Love of the Source **DIRECTLY** and **IMMEDIATELY** tangible here in the old, holy darkness.

Can you still remember how connected you were, wordlessly, in your childhood or youth, to the ALL-ONE Source of Love? You have come here in order to make this condition more consciously tangible. Language is an aid that was placed at your disposal—particularly the language of the heart! It is the language of the Source, the language of the Earth, the language of your own nature and the language of your deepest origins.

So many beings from different places in the Cosmos have come in order to agree on the same language—the language of the heart. At the moment, even all those that are here in non-physical form are actively taking part in this. Compared with your true wisdom, there is still a great deal of uncertainly and ignorance in your earthly knowledge. All this will be replenished with the knowledge of Love. You do not need anything more! You can take in information and pass it on more easily with the help of Love, if you want to do this. That is the language of Love. Love and vigilance lead you to a state of clarity. This is a state that allows you to see clearly just what lies within your possibilities.

Even those who at this time are not aware to what purpose they have come here, what their mission is on the Earth, who are at odds with this mission—EVERYONE has an effect with their service—EVERYONE is serving the All-One Source! Use the power of your heart—it will open all the doors to you!

Tomorrow, perhaps, you will already be a person with a totally different consciousness. Then you will know who or what induced you to change in this way. Only Love! It is the power that should move you, that should be your motivation for every action and utterance, for every thought and for every emotion.

We would like to tell you something funny about this change of consciousness: at the moment there is a big "product recall" underway. You surely know this expression from the car industry. The great cosmic product recall works like this: all attributes of the vehicle Man are now being repaired in the cosmic, intergalactic workshop of Love. Yes, there is a big recall and repair campaign. It is taking place on the Earth where all your aspects and attributes that prevent you from living in Love are being returned to the manufacturer, and for free, too! Perhaps you might just think for a minute in your state of worry, of depression, or of loneliness that you were recalled to the shop, in those conditions, to be "repaired." Yes, something like that is possible on the great planet Earth!

By means of the rapid development on the Earth, in recent times you have often been in the "workshop." Your vehicle is improving more and more in order to adapt to the traffic conditions here on the Earth. Yes, traffic here on the Earth is subject to continuous change. For that reason there is so much tinkering and re-installation being carried out on you. All this is happening in order to service your conveyance and its motor, to make it stronger, to iron out the dents in the body, and to fill it up with special fuel, of course. This fuel is the "Free Energy of Love." The special feature of your new vehicle is that you don't have to return for a refill for a very, very long time. One might say that your gas tank was altered. It was enlarged, and is now being filled.

We see that you are also looking forward very much to trying out your newly-repaired vehicle now, and to using it. Please remember as well that all the mechanics who have worked on your vehicle, and are working on it, do their work with perfect Love. Every single gesture is made in the highest of Love, and this makes your vehicle such a very special one.

We love you and thank you for listening to us! We wish all of you a great deal of love and a nice ride!

    Your Star Children

Divine Will—Kingdom

We greet you, our beloved, valued, strong earthly partner. We are with you during your entire journey of experience. Everything that exists is God's Will. Now you will perhaps ask yourselves, "God's Will? For God's sake! Are we truly helplessly at the mercy of the Will of God?" That is a good question. It leads you directly to the answer. **Yes, everything is the Will of God—you are the Will of God!** You arose out of the Will of God—you are the Will of God—you are the Will of God— you are the Will of God!

We sense and perceive what this feels like for you: how much has been set in motion within you in order on the one side to resist it, and on the other, to accept this old, familiar wisdom with relief. Yes, my child, you are the Will of God! Everything that you can see on this Earth is made for you. It is prepared for you and submits constantly to your inner intentions…and once again this great resistance against being considered a creator makes itself felt.

We are at your side because we are accompanying you lovingly to a special place—**to your throne**. We are with you in order to help you so that you can take a seat on your throne. What happens when you take a seat on this throne? As a king or a queen you will see that everything obeys your wishes. Your will and your wishes are carried out by your subjects. You can rule your kingdom in various ways. You can rule your kingdom so that either war or peace reigns. To take your place on the throne means to be in the middle of it all, to be at the center of your creative work, and to carry responsibility for your people. To take a seat on the throne also means to be energetic and powerful. This throne was prepared for you with great Love, care, wisdom and kindness. Wearing the crown often seems like a burden to you, doesn't it? It might appear easier to be a subject and to carry out the will of the ruler, to be acquiescent to him. Do you not see that both carry responsibility for one another? In order to rule, the sovereign has to have as much Love as all the subjects together. You can take on this role of crowned being with confidence, as it is not something new for you.

From your vantage point, you look upwards to your king. He does not look down on you, as he knows that you are a part of him and everything that happens to you, happens to him as well. Everything that he does affects you. At this point we want to lead you away somewhat from the dramatic way of looking at things just mentioned, as there really isn't anything dramatic about it—apart from the Divine Drama— the Divine Play that opens the eyes of the blind. Your well-being becomes the well-being of the king. The king's well-being becomes your well-being. You are caught in this piece of theater. You can sit down on the throne and take on the tasks of a ruler. In this way you can relieve yourself of the burden of being at the mercy of subjection. As you are committed to God, God is also committed to you. He will never let you down, because you and He belong together, because He gives his kingdom to you, because you were able to seat yourselves on the throne.

Divine power is the force of empowerment, the force of Love. You can join this power at any time, if you allow yourselves to see freely, that is, to accept all of your various views and perceptions of the truth and at the center of it all to allow the truth to simply BE. That is the state in which the king is at one with his kingdom, in which the kingdom is at one with its king. This kingdom is within all of you—all of you are this kingdom! You are ruler and subject—subject and ruler. In this kingdom there is nothing which does not express the Will of God. You see, in being his Will, you are God!

We are always with you, our dear friends!

    Your Star Children

The Beauty of Human Beings

We greet you, beautiful, radiant ones! We see your light, your charisma, your "power." It is so nice that you visit us again. Today we would like to speak with you about how beautiful human beings are. Human beings are born from the Spirit of God. Their Spirit is found in the joy in which we always reside. They are high, well-schooled beings in the service of Love. **They are deployed wherever Love is needed.** By means of their Love they possess the special ability to do this "very different work": earthly work.

There is so much Love needed to be able to slip into your human bodies and to play the Divine Game here. Not all who live in human bodies on the Earth are human souls. You are an eclectic group, here on the Earth. All have been given your bodies to use by Mother Earth. You human beings are chosen to carry to the Earth the great Love from which your Souls come. This Love is part of your baggage that you bring here with you, and leave here. You are beautiful, radiant beings who because of your special journey here—your service here on the Earth—have gone through a great deal of transformation. In order to play a special part here in the earthly game it is often a condition that you scarcely perceive your "True Light." Such special roles are experiences that you call pain. When seen from your plane of the Soul they are like a prison. Bringing about a change in this prison is what you and your many helpers are working on primarily, at this time. Your task in this life is to remove the prison bars from this prison! All who have come here for that reason are able to do it and will do it, as it is their mission.

The connection between your human consciousness and with your Soul, with the Spirit, is becoming more often possible, and in more intensity. In those special moments in which you perceive who you truly are, then you remove a prison bar from your prison. All this happens at the behest of the Divine, through the Love of the Source, through the Love of the Divine Mother, in order to serve the "bigger picture." As human beings, you perceive more and more that your activity on the Earth is a service to others. The others encompass the planet Earth. This encompasses everything that you call light and darkness. Everything corresponds to the Divine Plan. If you can see the Love behind it, it is easy for you to find your place within it and to exist in Love.

This means to be able to perceive, accept, and love the Soul behind the personality of the people in your surroundings and of all people in general. This will help you to free yourself from the role of the victim and the pain of human characteristics, and then to perceive here the light of the Soul, the spiritual origins, and the communal service being done by every being. If yesterday something in connection with another person still pained you, look today at the Soul of this person. See his spiritual task and that which is shown to you. Look to the Soul for what it will teach you—**your own Soul!** In this way it will be easier for you to continue and to find your way by the light of the Soul.

In times during which work on the removal of your prison bars is particularly intensive, all the helpers playing their roles of darkness in a very convincing way are those who have chosen a very special task for themselves. We would like to tell you that everything happens within the immeasurable Love and the Will of God the Father, of the Divine Mother. Those who make the "darkness" momentarily visible to you do this so that you can let go of this **suffering**—this darkness. Then you no longer need to remove it from within your Soul—then it will be taken from you. Such great Love comes from the Divine Source, from the Source of God. You are all heroes here! Every Soul has a special task for which it has come here, and to that end has chosen human consciousness.

We would like to give you an example of what the two possibilities of making something visible can look like. If you stand within the light, something can become visible to you if a shadow is created. Then it can be perceived by you and you notice it. If you stand in darkness, you can perceive by means of the light because it illuminates the site for you. Then you can see and recognize more easily. That is the Divine Cycle of Being and Becoming.

Divine Love is in everything. Everything flows towards you from the Source. You are a part of this Source. In these times we are standing at your side in a particular way, and it is a holy time. We ask you to open your heart for everything that happens so as to overcome the things that cause you suffering and to find inner peace more readily. If you exist in this Love, in this peace, in this center, then spread your powerful, graceful wings. It is good to see you in this greatness. Like solar panels, these wings collect Love and turn it into the Love that is needed here on the Earth. It is good to see so many of you already in this Love, to see into the greatness of your Soul. It is good to see you here in these hues. In this inner peace you are ready for everything that might arise.

We are with you in Love. You are with us in Love, we are at one in Love!

    Your Star Children

A Blaze of Color—Eyes of the Soul

We greet you, our beloved and valued brother—our beloved and valued sister!

God's Love is everywhere. Do you also see it like that? We would like to explain this to you in this way: God's Love is like a spectrum of colors. With your human eyes, you can see a very particular part of this multiplicity of colors. You can even make other sections of this spectrum visible with technical devices. You can also take in various colors with various possibilities from within this spectrum of colors. But you have yet another technical instrument integrated in the nature of your being which can perceive even more colors than the eyes with which you physically see. These are also eyes; we will call them **Eyes of the Soul**. They are a highly-engineered device, from a technical point of view, with which you can take in a much broader spectrum of colors than with your physical eyes.

And if God's Love is the richest and most varied range of colors that exists, then you can see with your physical eyes really only a particular section of it. With your Eyes of the Soul, however, you can see a much greater section of it. In that way you can see a much broader spectrum of God's Love with your Eyes of the Soul. You can probably imagine by now that there are no upper limits to the range of perception. The more you use the eyes of your spiritual connections, that much greater will your ability to see even more colors become.

In the course of your life you go through many experiences. Some of these appear as colors that you can see or recognize as such. Others vibrate in the colors of other frequencies that you cannot see with your physical eyes. Those are situations by which you feel surprised because you don't notice them right away as they are coming towards you, but only when they are right there in front of you.

We are speaking to you about the colors of God's Love. They are so diverse. You human beings can only see a small section of them. These colors are always in their full splendor with you. If experiences meet you in colors that you recognize, then these experiences are readily integrated into your being. These are experiences, or rather colors, that you can accept quickly and easily as you know within yourselves that these colors are from the Spectrum of Love of the Divine Source. On the other hand if experiences come to meet you in colors that you do not accept right away, then you do not yet recognize that these colors as well are found within the Divine Spectrum. You can recognize them with your soul's eyes, however!

Can you imagine how much more colorful your world becomes if you use the Eyes of the Soul?

When more and more becomes visible to you within the Divine Light, and you recognize it, the world will become more and more colorful and bright. If it seems brighter and brighter to you, then you can find your path everywhere, no matter where it leads you. Use the eyes of your Soul—we can also call them "Eyes of the Heart"—whenever it gets too dark for your physical eyes! With their help you can still see and walk clearly even in the darkness.

Thus we would like to invite you to use those Eyes of the Soul and to turn them into your physical eyes. And let your physical eyes become the Eyes of the Soul; let them become as one, and then you will always see from the perspective of your Soul, of your Spirit! If you have once seen with the Eyes of the Soul, then it is difficult for you to return to the old way of seeing. If you have once seen the wonderful blaze of color of the Divine Colors and of Love, the motor has been switched on that will lead you towards this spectrum of colors. Then, through the power of faith, you will all feel more at ease in this world. You will find fewer conflicts. You will perceive the healing Love that is in everything, that is in you, that you are. Your inner nature is made up of these wonderfully beautiful colors. Yes, those are the components of your most intimate nature, your Soul!

We would now like to invite you and others to try your new eyes. They help you to find peace. They allow you to perceive the Divine Presence in everything you look upon. And if you look in the mirror with these eyes, then you will recognize the colors of Love also within yourselves. With these eyes you can discover the divine array of colors in every corner of this Earth, search them out, and enjoy them. Your black-and-white film of life will become a technicolored one.

All these colors are present and stored in every cell of your body. You can always perceive that which you are. If you see the radiance of every one of your cells in the divine colors you can also recognize this in your surroundings. In this way you cause yourself and everything else that you perceive to shine, glow, and radiate. This is a further, very fine step that leads you into your true nature and that leads you home. You will also notice that you rediscover yourself in everything in which you can perceive to be Divine Light, and everything that recognizes you as Divine Light, you can also perceive to be Divine Light as well.

While you are absorbing these words, your vision within your ability to perceive is being sharpened by your loving, color-filled helpers on the radiant planes. Your inner lens is being polished, at this moment, so that you can recognize more and more easily who and what you are. We are with you with so much Love—we are in a state of great and wonderful joy because we may bring you this message! If you are confident enough to use the eyes of the heart, of the Soul, then you will recognize us. You will perceive us in a new form that is made up of finer colors than your physical images. Just allow it to happen! Let them appear within you! These are not images that you perceive as being at a distance from you; these are images that you perceive within yourself. We love you with our whole heart, as you are the same as we are and bring this Love, in this Love, to the Earth. We are holding your hand and communicating our thanks. Thank you for being where you are!

    Your Star Children

Wisdom

We greet you, our beloved and wise, wise workers on the Earth! Yes, today we call you wise, as that is what you really are, that is you! You not only recognize what you have to do here as the "work of the Soul," but you also have knowledge of the great ins and outs of the Cosmos.

We know how hard it often seems for you human beings to believe this pronouncement. Of course this is related to the fact that you are multi-dimensional workers that are active on many planes at the same time. You believe that everything happens on the plane of your human perception. Whether you perceive this consciously or not: on this plane you are always presented with the effects, the results, and the consequences of all your multi-dimensional decisions—that is how it is! Sometimes you make decisions on a higher plane than your human consciousness, as these are important for your education as a human being and as a Soul. These decisions often surprise you in your earthly consciousness. As you have already experienced, they can sometimes hit you hard. Please keep in mind that you have made such decisions by means of a consciousness linked to Love and Wisdom, as these are decisions that you intend to make. Then there are experiences wherein the impulse for them arises from "earthly attractions", even if the impulse for this has not been disconnected from your other planes of perception. This is important, as it has to do with the human view that the earthly plane of life is less "holy" than the spiritual dimension, the dimension of the Soul, your connection to the Source.

All these are various levels of perception. If you love yourselves, truly love yourselves, then you see the presence of the Source in everything, even on your earthly plane. In your earlier existences on this planet, you played various roles: a number of them may have involved the assessment and the judgment of one of the various planes. At that time, you felt yourselves to be even more separated in your earthly life from the Source, from the Consciousness of the Universal, and for that reason you judged things differently and considered various aspects of your human existence to be bad. The divine paradox within this is that God is in all dualities, is in **everything**. How could it be otherwise, if God is the source of all existence? For this reason we would now like to encourage you, all of you, to extinguish your cellular memory by means of Love, by becoming aware of this: everything streams from the great, single Source—God is in everything. This should change your entire set of values and the spectrum of your judgment.

The challenge of your existence is found in the fact that the various events of your life feel so different to you.

There are situations that come towards you in wonderful Love, and those which demonstrate to you your deepest fear and inner resistance. Resistance to what? Resistance to Love. You can overcome and undo such situations if you shine the light of Love upon them.

We are talking to you today about the untold wisdom that you possess. Your immeasurable wisdom gives you the possibility to hand something that is painful back to the Source again. As a human being, as Soul and Spirit, you are capable of this—as the Source! If you can accept that you are the Source, then everything streams out of you and back into you. You are the cycle, and maintain it. You are discovering the various planes of existence of this divine cycle. You are able to deal with seemingly difficult tasks because you can recognize yourself in them as their source and purpose.

All those who do their service on Mother Earth are led by her higher wisdom to transform the energy of this planet back into Love once more. We invite you now to feel your wisdom, to love it, to accept it—and to spend some time in it—to trust it, and to take your place in its embrace. Wisdom—that is a shimmering light, a shimmering color in your beautiful, multi-dimensional existence. It is a part of your nature, of the nature of all of you. As often as you wish, you can take the time to meditate on this wisdom, to enter into it and to linger in it. In this way it will extend as far as into your human thought.

We know in which way you are now, in these times, being charged with believing this, as wisdom can also show itself from its opposite side, in its duality, namely as futility and doubt. But only to tickle you a little, and to elevate you to your true greatness. Your earthly powers of perception are in comparison with your true nature of existence like a drop in the ocean. Every time that you are being tickled, see the antithesis! That turns the affair into something whole; it removes the illusion of being separated. If there was something in the spiritual dimension like illness, then it would be this illusion.

Our Beloved Human Being, all you Beloved Human Beings, all you Beloved Earthly Workers: our Love is with you! Your Love adorns and beautifies us. Your Love is an honor to us.

We are full of joy because of our Love!

>   Your Star Children

Sound

We greet you. It is good, the way that you are finding your inner channel. What is your inner channel? It is God's connection to you. It is the channel in which God lives and through which God speaks to you. This channel is a holy instrument, and every human being possesses the ability to elicit tones from this instrument in various ways. This channel is really an instrument which God plays! If you wish to listen to these tones, you have only to give yourself up to its sound. You have to open your ears and listen very carefully in order to hear the tones of this instrument. Divine Love knows your favorite music. God plays it, to get your attention, to get you in tune with the sound of the Divine. God enchants you with this sound. You can hear it in every aspect of your life. God plays such wonderful melodies and produces such a wonderful sound that it is easy for you to become aware of it at all times. This sound is the pure essence of Love. This sound is power in silence. This sound is endless space, omnipresence, and inner peace. This sound is the highest consciousness. This sound is All-Embracing Consciousness. This sound resounds within you! It is that which you should become aware of. It is that which allows you to become empty and free of all the extraneous details that you have been provided with in your life, in order to lead you once again to the most inward of sounds. This inner music has no space. You perceive it as sound within, although it is neither merely within, nor merely without; it is everywhere. However, you can most easily hear it deep, deep, within yourself.

Allow yourself to be delighted by this sound! This sound is the engine of your life! It is your true nature. Within this sound, with this sound, and by means of this sound you became a human being. It resounds in every cell of your body, in every single cell! And even stronger in the ethereal matrix, the ethereal counterpart to all your body's cells. This sound echoes in your reason, in your thoughts, but even more intensely in your creative imagination. This power of imagination is your longing for God, for yourself, for your deepest and truest nature. The entire game of life is SOUND.

**The way you are, the way you think and feel,
is the way you will sound.**

Sound connects you to everything that exists. Everything makes a sound! Everything that exists makes a sound. Nature, all living creatures, every planet and heavenly body in the solar system and in the entire Cosmos makes a sound. Allow yourself to be enchanted by the Divine Sound! You can find it everywhere. Why not begin your search right away, within yourself? This is the place that every sound in the Cosmos will lead you to. Your divine sound is creativity. Every being makes a sound in its own way within the total sound of "Everything That Is." Embark on a quest for your tone, for your sound, for the sound of your Soul! You will hear how beautifully you sound and how easily and directly you can hear yourself as a divine sound created by God. You are the sound of the Word that God speaks. You are the sound that emanates from God—you are the Sound of God. God has given you an instrument that plays His sound—it is your Soul! If you play this instrument, you produce divine sounds. You are a musician in the great orchestra, the great band, the great ensemble of God.

At times, this sound is very soft, as it wants you to listen very closely—very, very closely. Sometimes this sound is unmistakable, and then you know "where things are happening." In truth, it is this sound that energizes everything, which gives life to everything, which gives everything its consciousness, a consciousness that can appreciate its own sound within itself, as soon as it is created.

We want to remind you what a splendid sound, what a splendid melody you are, Beloved Child of Man, Beloved Human Being! It is good that you hear your own sound more and more clearly. It is good that you hear our sound. With our sound we break the sound barrier of the dimensions and bring this sound to you in order to encourage you to **also listen to yourselves**.

We resound!

    The Star Children

It is possible!

We are here and have been waiting for you. We want to show you how easy it now is for you human beings to perceive your multi-dimensional character. It is now already easier to change your states of consciousness. You can move through the channel more and more quickly that extends from human consciousness into all other planes of perception. This passage, this path between the forms of consciousness, is becoming more and more visible and easier to follow. You could also say it like this: "My Soul is walking towards me!" Earlier, it was advantageous for the plan here on the Earth not to be as flexible and open as it is now. It is much easier now, as you have given your permission on a spiritual plane for this to happen. It is entirely possible for you to move effectively through the various denser or lighter planes of perception. The longing to come home is very strong in most of you. Why? Because life as a human being can be very demanding, in a certain way. The word "demanding" contains "demand", and demand relates in a certain way to the inflexibility, the rigidity, in which your soul feels itself to be here on the earthly path, compared to that which is your true nature.

As has been mentioned, many are now pushing their way home, because they perhaps feel overwhelmed. And we tell you: in this case their work is finished! A number of them take the first opportunity they find to come home. That means, the Soul agrees to take the very first path towards home, on the physical plane, no matter what it may look like.

Of course all the various Souls feel "at home" in different places. We would like to explain this to you like this: in the course of your many human lives, you have often felt a longing to return home. Because of the great suffering on the Earth you simply wanted relief. Even if you haven't known where your journey was taking you, you have often simply wished to come away from here again. A number of you are also now longing to return to Love. There, those limitations do not exist which you know from life as a human being. A number of you still longs to go to another plane where you feel at home. And we want to tell you that for all the experiences that a Soul intends to have, **a suitable terrain will be made available by the Creative Source**. This depends on the Soul's wish, in precisely what way and how much individuality it wants to experience as an antithesis to the Universal Consciousness. Now, however, it is possible, in contrast to your memories of the Earth, to be "at home", to find security, comfort, and Love HERE—you can create it and express it here, and bring peace on Earth!

You are still so very much involved within human consciousness with struggles for or against something. It all depends on what you consider to be good or bad at that moment. Because of the particular demands of service on the Earth, particularly now a good many long for the world of the "good." We would like to remind you, however, that particularly now you have the ability to resolve this polarity. It is truly a special time in which you have come to this planet. It is now possible for you to achieve an awareness of your deepest origins, your nature, and your mission. It was not always possible to do this on the Earth. Now it is possible—now it is once more possible! It is now possible, in the great confusion of good and evil, not to have to search any more for an escape in one direction, but rather to re-establish unity.

We can see how your soul now rejoices in the knowledge that there is also meaning in the depths of dark experiences. Whenever you are confronted with something of enormity in your life, with a situation that seems to overpower you, then you now **no longer need to feel overwhelmed!** This situation is there to raise you to the same size as the challenge appears to be to you. **In such situations, there is also a part of you within it that wants to lift you up to the same size**. That is advancement! That is your path, and the meaning behind the illusions that are there for you in your earthly existence.

We say it once more: whenever you feel completely discouraged or consider yourselves entirely unworthy of being loved by others or yourselves, then it is a particularly loving part of you that is reflecting this situation to you, as it wants to shift you to the opposite of this perception. To the opposite, or we can also call it "resolution of a perception." One can also see it like this: this is God's plan, to show you once again the way out, to liberate you once again from the pain that you decided on beforehand. All of that lies within your power and within your nature, all that is you!

We invite you to look at the next challenge that you set for yourself in this way. Then it will be even easier for you to accept it.

If you find yourself in the state, in the consciousness of Love, is it not Love that you have to learn!

Do you know what we mean? Right there, where you do your service as a human being, you transform the consciousness that drew you to that place. You are the master who works there, who finishes his piece of work. It is you who can allow the piece to look as you would like it to.

You are truly blessed in your service; you are the blessing of your service! If you could only see what greatness a Soul needs in order to do that which it decided to do on this Earth! Beloved Child of Man, Beloved Being in service on the Earth. You are not that which you consider yourselves to be on this Earth. You are Love! You may gladly call your service "holy." How could you bring about change in this dimension, if it were not in you? How could you give Love, if that were not who you are? You are a gift for this Earth—all thanks to you!

We love you so much and are happy to be with you!

That is inner peace—that is peace!

    Your Star Children

Standing Still or Moving Forward?

We greet you! We greet you, Exulted Being! The veil is raised again and again. Do you sometimes feel like a loner? That is a sign of loneliness, a state that you are only capable of in human consciousness when you sense the presence of the veil particularly strongly. The veil was there in order to make service on the Earth even possible for you. Now, however, you are in a time here in which the established laws for earthly service have changed. That is the reason why the perception of creation for every person here on the Earth, without exception, has changed. Your Love is now returning to you again. It is on the way back to your human existence. At the moment, your consciousness is transforming itself more and more into a mediator between your earthly perception and your Soul—it is your connection to the Spirit. Earthly consciousness, which is normally very strongly influenced by sensory stimuli and memories, is acquiring an entirely new status. And it can sometimes happen that this part of your consciousness finds itself again in a crisis of uncertainty because it believes that it has lost its raison d'être.

It is just that way: the value and the quality of your earthly consciousness are changing at this moment. Instead of earthly consciousness being blotted out, it is taking on just the opposite: an even greater, more important, and more comprehensive status. Your higher levels of consciousness are expanding more and more easily into your earthly ability to perceive. That is also the reason why in this moment so many conflicts are taking place within your earthly consciousness. These are doubts about the meaning behind the various dimensions of existence in whatever form. This is part of the game—don't worry about this! If you should sometimes have the impression that you are losing your mind, just keep in mind that all your forms of perception, not merely the physical ones, are finding a new connection to one another. The passages between these levels of perceptions are expanding.

Earlier, partitions were built between these various forms of consciousness, and these partitions are now being dismantled. This is happening according to the way and the speed at which your Soul decides to open itself here on the Earth to a comprehensive consciousness. In the process, all the restrictive tenets and patterns of thought, all "former decisions" which consider this to be impossible, will appear for short periods of time. These patterns stem from times in which life here on the Earth had a different significance. Just go through this process of opening with confidence. Don't look for interpretations in your mind, but rather simply be open and it will reveal itself to you in a new form!

In the times in which you are living it is the physical nature of your existence, your earthly form, that is being worked on the most!

Your Soul, your spiritual origins, are active, in order to be perceived within the denser form of consciousness, as by means of the connection to it you can orientate yourselves to the center. Then, no matter where you are, you can move directly towards the center, towards your homeland.

That is the program and the plan for your deepest nature of existence. It can be helpful now if you pursue the wishes of your Soul and your heart, if you follow the inner longing of your heart and allow yourself to be led by this inner light. Keep in mind that you are on your way home! This inner light is your connection to the Source. It leads you particularly whenever you no longer know where this light is to be found, whenever you no longer know where you are; it leads you if the passing landscape on your way home has changed so much that you have no idea where on earth you are located. This connection to the Source is your navigation system. The destination has already been entered!

For this reason, be gentle to yourself on the way back home, and have faith if you travel through seemingly unfamiliar countryside that makes you fearful, that allows a feeling of isolation to arise within you. Keep in mind that the destination has already been programmed in! By whom?

By you! Everyone has entered his coordinates—even Mother Earth. Just have faith! The powers of attraction of the Source are so great that you cannot resist it and cannot miss your destination.

You find yourself in your vehicle that is taking you home. You can look out of the window now and admire the countryside and everything else that you see during the trip. You will meet people who are slower or faster than you, or who are traveling in groups. Everything is fine! Perhaps you meet groups of people who are apparently standing still, attracted by some event or other. Are you also going to stop? Perhaps in this situation there is a lot of excitement, there are by-standers, and many people who are attracted to it? Perhaps you would like to hurry over to help out in some way? Then take a good look! Do you see that everyone is on their way? Perhaps you are even one of them who are gathered around this event? Now take another good look, and leave your Love there! Perhaps you see in a number of them the light of their Souls which are close to their bodies and are ready to unite with them? Perhaps you recognize others as radiant Beings of Light among the many participants? Each person in this gathering finds himself on a particular plane of perception. On behalf of all the excited and curious spectators, beautiful, pure Beings of Light are present to help them to their own light once again. And perhaps you see other beings which have arranged that this crowd of people could come together? Can you comprehend their dignity with your human consciousness? That is the standpoint of all concerned, who are excited. Or can you manage it better with the consciousness of your Soul? That is the consciousness in which you drive past in your vehicle. Have a look at the possibilities you now have. You can of course spend some time in this situation, for as long as you consider it necessary. When you are able to recognize and appreciate who is doing what there, you will get into your vehicle again and set off on your trip home. A vehicle is waiting for each person whom you have seen at this gathering, to take him home.

You are so full of Love that you can unmask and recognize everything in yourself that resists going home as being a part of your earthly consciousness and earthly memory. In each of you there is so much Love that you were and are capable of taking on the most enormous roles, as human beings. Be who you are! Then you won't be judgmental, then you already see your home, then you are already at home!

Everything exists in Love! Do you like continuing the trip in this way?

We all exist in Love—Everything exists in Love!

Everything is possible—everything is possible—everything is possible!

   Your Star Children

Painting Class

Beloved Son, Beloved Daughter, we are with you! We thank you for doing your work so dutifully, often without knowing it. This does not mean that you have to do something particularly good. To do something noble means to follow your heart, as the voice that speaks from your heart is YOU. That is you on the level of your Soul, in the nature of your Soul as a Divine Spirit.

Now imagine a path that you are taking. This path, that is, the journey which you have set out upon as a human being, was drawn by you yourself beforehand. You as an all-knowing being in All-Embracing Love drew this path with Love. You indicated how wide this street or how narrow this way should be upon which you then as a human being are setting forth. You drew where the detours, the byways, and intersections would be. You drew the landscape, the natural surroundings, and the houses. You prepared all of this pictorially, neatly, and in the finest detail. And over and over again you concealed small details within this picture to remind you that you drew it, in such a way that you as a human being can discover the original artist by means of these special clues. You can think of this as a kind of "hidden secret code."

In many places you have added signs to it, some quite small and concealed and others as large as road signs. You have drawn the sun, which is to shine as you go along your path. And you have also drawn the moon. The sun illuminates your day and it helps you to see and to recognize things. It warms you and sends information to you from other suns, originating with the Ur-Central Sun. By this means, by means of these tiny particles, you can always receive necessary information from home. You did all of that well, and in a clever way! You drew Mother Earth as you will find her in your life as a human being. You drew all the mountains, valleys, meadows, and fields. You were forehanded enough to include soft moss which you can lie down on, so that you can feel the love and warmth of Mother Earth flowing upwards to you. Thus you have seen to it that the Earth's gentle vibrations of Love will cause you to vibrate in the finest way, as, just as the Earth vibrates, in a certain sense your body also vibrates.

You have also drawn water neatly. You have omitted no detail. You have drawn every single drop of water that is to fall from the heavens to slake your thirst and that of Nature. You have planned every single drop of water so that for instance the plants can grow. Every brook and every source, every little stream and every river, every tide and all the oceans, all bodies of water which you will meet in your life—you have envisaged all this pictorially in your picture.

"I really drew everything beforehand?" will be your question now. Yes—and with Love and great care! And as we already told you, it is now easier than ever to take up your creative brush. "But can I also change the drawing, too?" might be your next question. We would like to invite you to do the following: if there are "situations" in your picture that your human reason does not believe yourself to have drawn, **take a very close look!** You will discover a special detail! Pay close attention to this clue that you have left behind for yourself in order to discover yourself as being the painter. Somewhere, you have concealed a detail—it can be quite a tiny one—that helps you in the relevant situation and provides the key to the solution. In every situation you have all the tools that you need in order to master it in a loving way! You drew everything in there in finest detail. The only thing you have to do in this case is to look at everything in detail so that you find these tools, because they are there! You did not draw a single situation beforehand in which the solution to the task was not already contained within it.

]It is like a "picture puzzle", a picture where you have to find certain things contained in it. There is only one large difference to the picture puzzles that you are familiar with. When you have a human picture puzzle, you are told for example "Find eight errors!" In cosmic "picture puzzles" there are no errors! Your picture is perfect. The nice thing about it is that you have placed all the necessary details neatly and exactly there, where they should be, so that you can see and discover them. That is wonderful—you are such a great painter—you have created a gigantic picture of life! The paint and all the materials for it were given to you by the Divine Source. With this divine paint, you have painted yourself and everything else. The paradox is this: by painting on an empty page with divine paint you can recognize by looking at it that you are divine. If the colors depicting you on the paper and characterizing you are divine, then it can happen in no other way than that you recognize yourself as something godly. Divine recognition games are colorful and manifold—keep it in mind!

Imagine as a human being how wonderful all this is! Look at the wonderful things you have thought up in order to see yourself once again as divine. Thus you can rediscover that YOU can do everything, that everything is possible for YOU, that YOU are a part of everything and are at the center of everything.

We love you so very much and hope that you liked the divine painting class! We are to be found in the joy and delight which you felt within yourself in this divine painting class. We are with you. We are at any time with paint and brush at your side. Just call us, when you want to start to paint!

We love you, Divine Painter!

    The Star Children

A Secret

We greet you, our dear, sensitive, affectionate Creator of Worlds! We are happy that you are our friend! You see how easy it is to exist in our joy? We want to speak with you today about a secret. We want to confirm what you have already suspected. It is something whose veracity you will experience when you exist in this joy. It is also something you search for if you do not exist in this joy. This secret is a message for all human beings independent of what path they are on, independent of whether their path is particularly spiritual or particularly secular. The highest goal in life is: **you don't have to be anything!**

For many of you, a large, oppressive stone now falls from your heart. Many Souls now rejoice when they hear this. What does that mean—not to have to be anything? Every time that you think you have to do something remarkable or special to please God, then this motivation arises from an awareness that something is lacking. This is an inner state that your Spirit is not familiar with. In order to simplify this, we would like to talk about this a little. Whenever you think you have to do something special to fit in with a group of people or even a whole society, then you cut yourself off in that way from the Universal Consciousness. There is a lot of motivation and drive in this intention, and of course the impulse to do this arises from out of a lofty motive. But through this way of behaving you always fail to see who you are. Every human being can perceive a connection to the All-Embracing Existence if he accepts himself as he is.

Many people try to adhere in all aspects of discipline to the spiritual communities to which they belong. This dedication is, of course, blessed.

However, with all this discipline they can learn a great deal from people who can accept the holiness and splendor of the moment. You don't have to contribute anything special if you want to achieve a connection with your Soul, with your Spirit. It is of course the aim of many to be the best they can possibly be in everything they strive for, whether it is in their profession, in their religion, or in the role that they see as ideal for themselves. To have an ideal and an aim is of course a wonderful motivation.

The trick to pull off in these times is, however, to employ a method that can liberate you in every situation in your life—an awareness that can fill every moment in your life with Love. To dissolve into the bliss of the moment, you only have to know that you don't have to be anything special! As we already said, you practice being particularly good at your many different kinds of roles, for example. Others are very good in their efforts to be bad. Many are very good at being able to see themselves as losers, as all of those are earthly ways of reacting to coming in contact with the Soul. These are all earthly memories from your many experiences on the Earth, as your consciousness knew no other way to react to the separation from the Universal Loving Consciousness than to take up a particular role. The pain at the loss of the soul and spiritual connection was so great that you often took on roles that reconfirmed this pain again and again. In that way the result was reconfirmed and recreated anew: "Yes, it's true that I am insignificant and unworthy." Earthly consciousness did not even dare any more to search for its true origins and to enquire about them.

You are now living in a time in which all these patterns are dissolving. If you don't have to be anything special any more, then you can be everything that you want to be, within your heart—then you are everything. That is a valuable key that you can all make use of right away. You can open the prison of earthly illusions with it. Open the door and liberate everything that is longing for the Light! Every earthly illusion arises from your wanting to be and do something special in order to raise yourself out of the earthly. We want to give you this mantra that you can constantly repeat for as long as you need it.

The goal in life is to no longer have to be something!

Just be the person that you are at this moment, and do nothing to make this something special!

We would like to remind you that our beloved Jesus and all those seen as great saviors who have provided so many impulses for so many people over thousands or hundreds of years, did not try to do anything special in their lives. They knew that the greatest goal was simply to BE. You can achieve this with or without any technique that you have perhaps practiced in your life. Simply be who you are, in awareness, not having to achieve anything special, as the special thing that you do achieve by this is inner freedom! It frees you from the work on the assembly line of the usual human intentions and reactions.

Beloved Friend, we love you so much—and this is no special Love! This is the Love that connects everything, starting from the Great Source and ending in the Great Source. We are all a part of this Love. We are a part of this Great Entirety, component of this Great Entirety, the enterprise of Love, this Great Entirety, the firm of Love. It is above having to be good or evil, friendly or unfriendly. This is the Love that keeps all the answers ready for you. This Love is the way, the path, that leads you home—that will welcome you in your entirety when you arrive home. We invite you to bless the next situation that you create as a challenge for yourself with this mantra that we have given you. The highest goal in life and in spirituality is: **not to have to be something!**

We love you, Great Changer of Worlds! All of us are with you—we are holding hands with everyone in the knowledge of who we all are. We thank you for your Love in endless respect!

The Star Children

Elohim

We greet you, beloved and valued confrère. "You call me a confrère?" you will probably ask now. Yes! We want to tell you today how valuable every attempt is that you human beings have undertaken since the beginning of time to come closer to God. It was already a special feature of the Cosmos that so great and lofty beings took on human form and then kneeled in longing and prostrated themselves on the ground before God, in this form, as in order to be effective on the Earth, you left your light-filled garment at home. Now you can recognize two aspects in regard to this matter.

Firstly: how a being feels who does not entirely remember the close relationship to the Source and, secondly: just how much Love and devotion this other part, which is close to the Source and the All-Embracing Consciousness, possesses in order to be able to give himself up to the experience of individuality.

The part that languishes here on the Earth will again and again make an attempt, out of the deepest intuition and the deepest desire, to re-establish the connection to the Source. In this way you have passed through all religions, have prayed to God, have pleaded from within the deepest part of you that your hardships might have an end. You have cried out: "God, give me a place at your side! What do I have to do, to attain this?" This longing for your true nature had on the human side so much disappointment and pain as a consequence, that you sometimes simply decided in favor of the pain. You then concentrated more and more on this pain, as re-connecting to the Source of Love showed itself to be so arduous, and the pain at not being at home was so great. Then you considered pain to be God! You used pain as a pretext, as then you did not have to think about the longing, as sometimes it is easier for you to undergo the pain of separation than to close the gap of separation with the consciousness of Love. Thus, you felt pain to be the means and the purpose of earthly existence.

It carried you for many lives, and confirmed and supported the feeling of having been banished from Paradise. At the same time, however, it was a symptom of your longing to return home. NOW, though, you have the opportunity to re-establish the connection to the deepest Source quite easily, much more easily than before. You don't need to let pain confirm any longer for you how lost you all are!

If in earlier times you had a secular or religious position of leadership and spoke about this pain, it happened very quickly that you had many on your side who confirmed this. Thus the most imaginative techniques developed as ways to cause oneself pain and to perceive isolation and loneliness as the only reality. Only when the pain reached its peak was there salvation—the permission to reconnect to the Source; only then, when you couldn't stand it any longer and the pain had crossed a threshold of intolerability on the physical or spiritual level. Now you bless all of this, and your cellular memory, that stored all of this, is dissolving! God loves you so unutterably that He always gives you the opportunity of connecting to Him no matter how far away from Him you feel yourselves to be. God has always kept the spark of connection and recollection alight even in your most isolated consciousness, as your spiritual connection to the Source remained always on the other side, beyond the blockade.

And everyone who has climbed down into this darkness has done service and achieved great things, as there he will be a reminder of the whole! Now is the time in which everyone is remembering the whole and bringing the consciousness of Love to the planes of the most distant illusions of separation. This is what we mean by **extinguishing cellular memory**.

There is so much love in every single human being among you that you can illuminate entire worlds with it.

Please look at yourselves once under this aspect, and let it work within you! A time now prevails in which this grief due to having been banished has ended. Now is a time for joy and salvation. It is accomplished! You are the Source that has accomplished everything. Let yourselves be led by your heart; then you dare to be Divine Beings on the Earth once again, because as Divine Beings you have no limits. The Love, the Will, the Power of the Divine Father, the Divine Mother, the Divine Source is within you, IS you! All the reasons to feel insignificant have dissolved away.

Do you understand now what we mean when we say that all your efforts to long for the divine on the Earth are blessed? Nothing is in vain. You were the bringers of light on all levels of BEING into which you made your way. You went into the darkness to spread the Good News for yourselves.

Beloved Brothers and Sisters. That is what you are doing right now. That is what is happening right now. That is what you are doing with such dedication and what is happening right now in Love. We feel such great joy because we can admire you in this great service. Do you see what wonderful beings you are? Can you see your own service? Wherever you serve, you bring blessing! Your service is blessed. Now the essence of your true nature has also penetrated your human consciousness. This is a wedding celebration. Celebrate this marriage now, every day, every hour, every moment! That is the meaning of your existence. In this consciousness you radiate in the most wonderful light and play of colors that the world has ever seen. The Earth gives thanks and greets you with the same colors, the same light.

This is the Good News from the Source, into your heart. We love you, your power, your devotion, your entire being, just as you are!

Elohim! The Star Children

Hate

So you would like to know how to deal with the painful energy of hate? Hate, what is that anyway? Hate is one form of expression of Love! Hate is employed as a cosmic force everywhere that Love tries to make itself felt in a very particular way. When Hate and Love meet one another then you have the opportunity to recognize them with your consciousness as two sides of the same coin. Now all of you will say: "There is no greater contrast than hate and love. How can they be one and the same thing?" From out of the Love of the All-Embracing Source we say to you that love and hate are simply like two different languages.

Because you perceive yourself in your strivings as an individual, moving seemingly further and further away from the Source, you meet various manifestations of fear on this journey. A "very concentrated form" of fear is hate. What happens to you, if you feel hate? On the human level, hate leads to destruction—and in the end even to the destruction of that which you hate. Destruction? Isn't there once again a key to the Cosmos within it? Might this key not be that in this way the awareness of being separated and the loneliness that you have created in order to confirm your isolation from the Source, is once again destroyed?

Hate holds many cosmic aspects within it. It is a great challenge for you human beings, because it is so strongly linked to fear. For that reason you don't dare to look at and recognize your own hate. If you recognize the aspect of cosmic Love within hate, however, you give yourselves the opportunity to meet this force and to look at it.

Just imagine now that all the hate that you have amassed piles up in front of you. Even if you can't see it like this at first, just imagine nevertheless Love at the core of this image. The core carries this energy, as hate alone could not exist. Take up a secure position at a distance from this hate, and just walk around it. Look at this construct. How does it look? What is hate saying to you? What does this feel like to you? Can you recognize that this hate does nothing without you, that its core is subservient to you? It is meant to help you to destroy and break apart what you have made out of it. How much courage and Love will you need if you come close to hate? You shouldn't merely look for the lowest kind of emotions within, but the exact opposite as well: **the cosmic intention with which you came in order to redeem yourself.**

Hate is a tool for those who have created powerful stereotypes of their enemy. They will then destroy these stereotypes by means of hate again, as in truth the deepest inner space, the holiness of one's own being, is walled up by all those who hate. These stereotypes of the enemy that have been created—they embody the illusion of being separated from the Source—will be destroyed by this hate. That means that hate is one of the greatest manifestations of the longing for the Divine Source! Aren't you relieved? Hate holds sway there where the longing for your deepest Love has become unbearable. Hate is a vehicle that those have need of whose longing for God has become unbearable. What should a human being do, if the hate becomes greater and greater, if it spreads to everything and everyone, if it goes so far that there is nothing more and no one else left, that one could still hate? Then HATE will destroy itself! That is its mechanism, and the way this energy works.

This is a particular energy that can come to fruition and be experienced here on the planet Earth. A suitable terrain is placed at the disposal of all beings who wish to experience it by All-Embracing Love. And just as EVERYTHING is an expression of cosmic Love, hate is as well. You now have the possibility of recognizing this!

We would like to invite you in addition to recall various aspects of hate. Begin with the limited human view of hate and move on to ever-larger, broader, and comprehensive perspectives until you can see everything that this energy contains, as hate is such an intense energy of Love, reduced to one point, that it has an explosive effect. We can see and admire how you confront this topic as human beings—where you as spiritual beings know and love everything! You are such special beings!

The experiences of your Soul have confronted you with all of that. The particular aspect of your times is that the Love stemming from the All-Embracing Being, the All-Embracing Will, and the All-Embracing Clarity are making themselves felt on your planet. On your planet! **In that case, there is no possibility for hate to conceal itself within the human way of looking at things.** Everything is raising itself up to the divine dimension that you are. You are now capable of looking at everything from the perspective of Love. That is your task, that is your way forward, that is your Love!

As human beings you can say: everything is becoming Love.
As Divine Beings you say: everything is Love.

We love you the way you are, just there, where your consciousness now finds itself on the great and wonderful journey. We love you so much and thank you for that which you have taken upon yourselves. You are the great bringers of change. You are the great loving ones. You are the Light in the name of the Great Source!

The Star Children

Letting Go — Emotion

eloved!

We come in a gorgeous light to you. This inner impulse that you sense is us! Yes, that is us! We want to show you how easy it is to let go.

You are all familiar with situations in which you are asked again and again to let go. This demand on you is particularly strong if powerful feelings are involved. Well, emotions are something unique to your earthly existence. Emotions are like a gigantic movie screen. They help you to recognize yourself as an individual throughout your experiences and your various mental states. Emotions are something quite different for you as human beings from what they are for you as Divine Beings. It is emotions that shape your life so strongly here on the Earth. Emotions are what often force you human beings to stand still because they personify your identification with a portion of the whole. Emotions can make you addicted. They function as a kind of substitute for your true nature.

We would like to explain the following to you: for a being that corresponds to your true nature it is a sheer impossibility to go through experiences the way you do as a human being. **On the Earth you have the opportunity to make do with a portion of the Great Consciousness**. In the moment in which you identify with something and through that, move into duality and one-sidedness, you are connected to emotion. According to the intensity of the identification of this one-sided part, you will attach yourself with emotion to this part until the other side of you gains recognition as well. Thus, emotion is a tool for doing so. It allows something that is as tiny as the head of a pin to appear gigantic to you. It expands your views of things on this giant screen. And the larger this screen and the image are, that much more are you convinced by what you see.

Now, these emotions are very closely connected to the physical body. They affect your body when they enter it and affect it, when they leave. Entering is quite easy because in your earthly existence you long for the other side, for your true nature, and many emotions serve as a substitute for these for you. If you want to focus once again on the whole, however, you need to "see through" these attractive images, that is, to let go of these emotions. And as difficult as this is for you as a human being, that much easier is it for you as a spiritual being. Use your true nature, your Divine Origin, to be rid of these illusions! As a human being you probably experience this as a loss, having to let go of emotions, because you do really give up something that has touched you physically. Your physical and emotional bodies are closely connected to one another. As a Spirit, as a free Spirit, however, this is something natural to you, as you know that every one-sided view of consciousness and perception detains the Whole.

Good, we want to help you to let go of emotions. If you are suffering under the weight of intense emotions, when you are afraid or are depressed, try to look at it this way: it is you in fact who are holding on to this, who is holding on to the cord!

It really is like a cord being pulled from both ends. You have the one end firmly in your hands and hold onto it tightly. You can truly free yourself from lesser and greater emotions and really liberate yourself by now letting go of this cord. Let go! In that way your identification with the one-sided quality of the issue that was connected to this emotion will dissolve. You can then see how much energy is available to you for everything else that you would like to do. If you let go of one cord after another, you can tap into all of your energy, and are unbeatable.

We would like to offer you yet another explanation, another piece of information, regarding this screen. There, where you are connected emotionally to something, if you are holding on to it, emotions are projected onto this enormous screen and appear to you in your duality to be reality. For this reason, many do not even consider letting go of these emotions, as they are standing in front of so many projected and attractive images. But you can simply turn the projector off by letting go of the cord, as then this projector has no more electric power.

Everything that you think, you wish for, you long for, is projected onto this screen by your projector and creates dependency. Of course, part of you now resists letting go of this, the part that considers these memories to be true and uniquely viable, as it believes it is losing everything. Yes, it believes that it has simply lost. With your deepest spiritual perception, however, you see how richly you are rewarded, if you give this up, as all this has stopped up or blocked individual channels leading to the giant channel of Love. Be courageous, and let go! That is surrender, but not surrender to something unfamiliar that demands a sacrifice from you. It is surrender to yourself, to your true nature, to your true greatness, to your limitless Love. How do you like letting go of your cord? You can start with a very small cord, then another one, and another one. But it is just as easy to let go of the large ropes, as in that way you become greater, broader, stronger, and more powerful. Now everything is possible.

Just a hint regarding letting go. Just feel the cord, how you pull on it in its "entanglement", how forcefully and stubbornly you're holding on to it, how narrow it makes you feel. Feel it, and then let it go—let it go! With that, all the images, convictions, and opinions that you have drawn to yourself dissolve into thin air. A number of them climb up to the sun and burn in the cosmic fire of Love. Others stumble into the water and dissolve into their original components. A number fall to the Earth and shatter and break. Everything has been liberated again! You human beings are the ones who do this service, who are capable of releasing this suffering. Your Divine Consciousness brings this about. This is you. You are the important workers on the Earth that are capable of it. Let go, and you exist in the indescribable Love in which we exist with you!

We love you ineffably! Our Love cannot be described in words! It is beautiful to see you liberated!

In Love

    Your Star Children

Inner Direction—Inner Godliness

We love you! We admire you! You will go down in history as a great master—as someone whom you can admire as a human being, as everywhere to which inspiration draws you, you do your service. Sometimes it is easier for you human beings if your spiritual presence takes over the leadership. All of your life's tasks come towards you with varying degrees of attraction. If there are experiences that you absolutely intend to have then it is your deepest inner guidance that leads you into these opportunities for learning. In this way you can again see what multi-dimensional beings you are. You are never alone, never forsaken, never helpless. Your spiritual dimensions are always at work so as to bring you back entirely into Love—to connect you with Love.

Sometimes it is right and necessary that you feel a longing for your divine nature. Then you will move in this direction, as you want to experience completeness. In this way, this need appears to have been met, for the time being. Afterward, a new plane opens up that wishes to unite completely again with Love—to give itself to Love. Here on the Earth you are in a continuous cycle, and thus you always move in the right direction. Isn't it sometimes a little eerie for you, how readily the "other" dimensions open up for you?

You are everything! Everything that you do, everything that you ask for, is you!

What might that mean? That there is no other power in the Cosmos except the All-One, driven by Love! All actions arise out of this power. Everything arises from out of this power, every being and every creature.

This is like a large, a very large family that at its core knows that it is one, a family in which one member knows what the other one is doing, in which one member knows how the other one will react. Now you have come to this planet with many of your "relatives." It is your presence that is leading the Earth into a special state. **Mother Earth is also a part of your large family**. She is not of a different species. You have agreed beforehand just exactly what you will do here in your present earthly life.

You are such a high and beautiful Spiritual Being.

Your earthly consciousness, that is your ability to remember everything that you did on the Earth, is always a little afraid of that which you really are. On the one hand it is incomprehensible to you, and on the other hand it is good that you discover your true identity in stages, as otherwise great confusion would arise in human reason. Perhaps your reason would create new feelings of guilt if it realized all at once who you really are, and if it always had to compare your divinity with the experiences that you plague yourself with here on the Earth. For this reason your spiritual connection always makes its way, further and further, as far as your lowest, that is, your superficial consciousness. Then you give yourself a chance, as a human being, to grow into that which you really are, as on the earthly side you are meant to present all the experiences that you have had to your deepest Divine Being.

You can take everything, every experience, and hand it over to your deepest Truth. In this way you strengthen your confidence in yourself, knowing that every action that you have carried out and carry out now, is a divine action. In you—through you—no lesser being than God takes action. Now you could ask: "If God acts through each of us and through everything, why do the people here on the Earth behave in such contradictory ways, some out of Love and some out of suffering? **Because all these deeds and experiences are experiences that are subordinate to, and are, experiences of Love.** There are no barriers, no constraints, and no limits to your Divine Consciousness. That means that your life is divine! Thus your earthly life as well suddenly takes on a divine dimension. If you want to be active here on the Earth, and to be so throughout many lives, then it is appropriate to take on a human body—and this is God. We now call this level of experience "Divine Level of Experience", for the first time. How should your reason understand otherwise what you are doing here? Of course it is on the one hand God who is in the spiritual dimension. Up to now you have perceived that you are on the other side, the opposite or the opposing side, to God. That is dual consciousness. But it is no contradiction, as:

Even in this world God's experience is infinite and limitless.

Of course it was easier throughout the long periods of earthly existence to look for God only on the other side, the spiritual side. This was a reliable and important tool, so that you weren't fettered for too long here on the Earth. Do you understand what we mean? It was simply safer and better to keep changing you back, again and again, into the other form of perception. This is possible through death. You can also perceive it without death, particularly now. If you had remained in your "times of earthly beginnings" too much longer, the longing would have kept on growing, in a certain way; in that way you would have been burdened with more and more longing and identified with it, instead of with the Love of the All-One.

You exist in the midst of your Divine Presence and have put on human armor for this work here on the Earth, as this place is a special arena of experience, in which there is a fight taking place. Here, the Divine Consciousness expresses itself in a very particular way. Now, however, you are here at a time in which you find yourself in the process of laying by your armor, as it is needed less and less. This place is transforming itself through you and with you. This, the Earth, is the place in which divine beings have given themselves up to the consciousness of duality. You can imagine this quite easily in this way: perhaps someone or other created and prepared this place in ages past as a place to experience duality. Now you have come, you have all come—by your presence this place is being altered. Perhaps there is then an entirely different place which is responsible for experiences that are "Earth-similar" ones.

This place, your Earth, is now becoming a place to live where duality belongs to the past. Can you imagine how much Love is needed for that? All the old cellular memories that were created because of and with the help of duality are being dissolved. Thus your body is also changing very rapidly now. Your armor is losing its rigidity, as you don't need it any more.

God is in this world through you. You are in the right place! It is God's wish that you are here. This conforms to His Will, His Joy, and His unconditional Love. We invite you to stroll through the world and to perceive everything that you experience from your divine vantage point. Then you can rejoice in Love, which is in everything, as well—in everything that you see and hear and do and don't do—in nothingness. Unconditional Love is in everything, in what you see and in your eye itself, otherwise you could not see this Love; in your brain, where this image arises, in all your senses, which interpret this image. Hand over everything to your Inner Godliness! In that way you unite yourself with the cosmic force of Love that can make everything happen.

We thank you for listening to us. We love you and everything that you do, everything you think, everything you feel. We love you!

    The Star Children

The Source

We greet you, our beloved, radiant star! You are the light of the Cosmos. You are the Love of the Divine Source. We greet you. It is good that you receive us in Love. We have waited for you. We have waited for you in the condition you are longing for: Love—this is our place of meeting, our venue.

We want to tell you today that you are a creature of God. All right—somehow this isn't news to you anymore. But today we want to tell you that the words "God" and "Man" are becoming more and more similar in their meaning. In earlier times you could say much more readily, "I am a human being, and God is God." Then many of you did allow it, more and more often: "I am God—I am the Creator," as long as things went well for you. However, this is now the time, the phase, of your cosmic recollection, in which you become aware that you ARE God.

We love you so much! We know how much good it does you when you feel this Love, as then you feel us—then you feel God, the Divine Source—then you feel yourself. It is all ONE. The Love of the Source—what does that mean? Today you get an answer!

The Love of the Source is YOU!

You are capable of everything—in the Love that you are—because you are everything. Because you are everything that exists! You are the core of Creation. **"You are the most beautiful thing I have created,"** thus speaks the Source to you! **"You are the most beautiful ray of light that I have created. You bring light to the Earth."** This ray of light touches everything that longs for it. It has the gift, you could even say the quality, of devotion, of throwing a Divine Light on everything, or of shifting everything into Divine Light. It can touch everything on this planet with Love and light.

In order to be able to penetrate into every place where you are needed, you slipped into the appropriate disguises and wore the greatest variety of costumes, as then you would be accepted there, where you were called, where you were needed.

Beloved Star Child! You are one of us! You are the radiant star that shines on the Earth—just as we shine in the heavens. You are the warmth that many long for. You are the cooling breeze that many long for. You are the Love of the Father that many long for. You are the Love of the Mother that many long for. You are your own redeemer that you long for, because the Source reigns and works within you, because your name is a hymn of praise, because your joy is to heal, because your Love is Divine Presence—for your courage is light, peace and devotion—for your courage is the courage born of the longing for your true presence.

When we say, "We love you!" then we want to elevate you to your own power, to lift you up. Now, in this holy moment, you are capable of recognizing the Love of the Source as your Love. Resistance is fading, fear is falling away, fear is transforming itself into Love! All your wishes are focused on one thing, and this is your heart—and **"your heart is my heart,"** says the Great Source!

Beloved Brother, Beloved Sister on the Earth!

"I am always with you. I have your back. I am happy with you. I struggle together with you. I weep with you. I feel Love with you. Use your wings, as they shimmer in my luster!" Beloved Ones on the Earth, all you Beloved Ones—we feel such joy! With this joy we are permitted to deliver the sound of the Source to you today! We are also holding a mirror in front of you—that shows you your true face—the way you look as cosmic ambassadors of Love. You are gorgeous. You glow in the light of the dawn. You are the freshness of the morning dew. You are the strength of the noonday sun. You are the joy of the evening and the peace of the night.

You Dear Ones, today we have done our work well as for every one of you, a spark has flared that allows us all to glow within the same Light. We are one. These are no longer abstract words and ideas. Finally you may say it out loud: **We are one, we are all taking part in the service of Love!**

We love you! Your beauty is our raiment, your gracefulness is our joy, and your Love is our highest goal. Your heart is our treasure. Your will is our devotion. Welcome to the new Earth! We love you! Can you see the Spirit of God in everything—in Nature, in every plant? You are the rose in the Divine Garden, if you wish to be. Love is your origin—Love is your mission—Love is your goal. There is Love in everything that meets you. We thank you and love you; we have every reason to do so: because you exist! You are important as a human being. You are rightly a cosmic being. You, as God, are Love.

You have the ability to embrace the entire planet. You have the power and the Love to let the entire solar system exist lovingly within your heart. We wish you all the best as a human being! We wish you as a human being Love, clarity, and the courage that your true nature possesses. All that you are, we are, too. And all that we are, you are as well. You are the salvation—you are the solution for this planet.

Remain as open as a Star Child!

> Your friends, your many-hued and light-filled Star Children.
> We are brothers and sisters, if you want to look at it that way as a human being.

Health

We greet you, our beloved friend! Do you know that you are a tower of strength? Do you know that you are healthy? Health and illness are two very interesting aspects between which you move, here on Earth.

Do you think that your Spirit, that is, your connection to the Divine, can become ill? No! That which you feel as illness might best be described as adjustment difficulties. Adjustment difficulties—what does that mean? You are a multi-dimensional being. Even as a human being you are not made up of merely your physical body. You also have other energy bodies in, around, or close to your physical body that all interact with one another. All of these various bodies vibrate at different frequencies. One could say that each body vibrates at a certain speed, that is, each body has the ability to settle into a certain frequency of energy. **Every body vibrates at its own frequency and can only take on certain frequencies.** Thus, when taking on energy from the outside, the actual pattern of vibration of the respective energy body is altered. You can perceive this for example in the case of thoughts or feelings.

Only your physical body is composed of different frequencies of vibration. Every unit in your physical body, every assemblage of cells that creates either a corresponding organ, a type of muscle, bone, or nerve, your brain, or whatever else it presents itself as, vibrates at correspondingly different frequencies. You could make each of these frequencies audible, as a tone, and then you would hear the symphony of your body. Your bodies with finer energies vibrate on the other hand at other frequencies—they vibrate at a higher frequency. In that way they cause the physical body to react accordingly. That is how this "guidance" functions from within the level of your thought, and that is how your physical body reacts to emotions and your mental attitude.

Physical illness comes about if the interaction between these bodies becomes disharmonic—if one of the interactions between these various bodies is too domineering. All these bodies are connected, impinge upon one another, and can influence one another interchangeably. Like a pyramid, the hierarchy of energy is most easily controlled by the finest energy, that is, from the top down. All right, how does such a state of disharmony come about? It arises if one of your bodies takes in more energy than it can handle. Energy moves around, flowing through your various bodies. It flows through your various bodies and stimulates them. If this energy stops somewhere, the basis for what you call illness is created.

We have already spoken about this standstill and what causes it in you. Events or situations that affect you strongly can cause blockages of energy such as this. So that your physical body continues to function, however, there is an instance within you that wants to keep this whole system up and running. It sees to it that disturbing energy is "ignored." If one of your other bodies, whether it is the physical, emotional, or some other one, allows itself to be particularly affected by a situation, so much so, that an "impression" comes about in the channel of energy, then this flow of energy is interrupted. Your inner sentinel, however, wants the entire system to keep going and will help you to ignore this injured area.

This sentinel will pull in as much energy from the whole system as is necessary to isolate the injured area and will build substitutions and workarounds for it. This is a well-functioning survival strategy for your physical body. If the places that need repair increase more and more, however, then it will cost the entire system so much energy that its ability to function will be impaired. Now you will ask, "How can one repair these injuries, these bruises completely again?" That is a good and important question—**through the power of Love!**

In your most ethereal body an energy vibrates that does not allow itself to be influenced and injured. It is so to speak a "heavenly instance." You can make use of its power at any time and use it to repair the injured areas. This is happening on an energetic level even now, while you are reading this, while you are finding hope. Your deepest energy, your deepest power, help you to tear down the protective walls and the barbed wire fence around the injuries. This takes place with insight and Love. Then the energy can flow freely again. It doesn't have to be re-routed anymore. You now have all the energy that you expended in order to hide the injury once more in its entirety at your disposal for that which you really want to do.

You came to Earth with so much Love—this Love is at your disposal for healing work on yourself, on your physical body. Now we would like to tell you about this energy of Love. You can use it in order to expose and take away all the "replacement parts" that were necessary during "first aid." You yourself have the power to bring yourself into a freely-flowing condition once more. Everything that exists in the Cosmos as energy is at your disposal. At times you have used this energy pretty successfully against yourself, when you forgot who you are. Now you can use this power once again and in that way bring clarity and Love to your whole system of energy. Yes, you have the power! You are this highest instance which can make use of all these possibilities. Everything that you need to do it is at your disposal, until your physical body knows no illness anymore.

Yes, that is how your energy system is organized. Everything flows—and if there are problems somewhere, the repair team goes to work right away in order to protect you from them. The payment this repair team asks of you is energy. You can dismiss this team from its work if you "unmask" your own, true origins. Then you will notice that in truth you don't need any protection. Everything is possible now!

Let the energy flow gently from your Higher Self down into your physical body.

Your physical and your fine-energy bodies have a huge capacity for storage. By means of this Love you constantly alter the information, the data, in this storage space—Love is your proper programing.

Your greatest challenge facing all that are your feelings of guilt, and you can trace all the pain that you human beings feel back to one thing: you took on this guilty feeling when you came to this planet. You took it on by becoming a human being. It came from the pain of losing your true nature. Now, this guilt is resolved within you! It fulfilled its protective function for all your earthly energy and is not necessary anymore. The entire energy of this protective function has transformed itself back into the free energy of Love that you are now absorbing into your being.

This protective aspect had the task of justifying your earthly service because you didn't remember your true nature. You are on a great journey—that is a true adventure. You are so courageous, so powerful! We admire you, every one of you, your dedication, as what YOU are doing is writing a new chapter in your universe, your galaxy, and wherever…

Your true nature has nothing to do with illness—it doesn't know illness—you are not ill! Can you accept that? Let yourself be drawn to the Light that you are!

We love you!

    Your Star Children

Evolutionary Step

We greet you, our loving representative from the Stars! Yes, you come from the stars! Up there in the heavens, where the stars shine brightly, there is your true home. Your light, which you embody here on Earth, radiates from there.

You are a thought of God! A thought of God? What on earth is meant by that again? A thought of God? Just imagine it like this—God thinks, "It is important that you are here on the Earth." At this moment "a lot" is happening on the Earth at the same time. In the particular kind of activity that predominates here on the Earth, you not only see the effects of your "critical" actions but also the results of your divine actions. To put it another way: all of you that dwell on the Earth—and that does not exclude the Being of Mother Earth herself either—find yourselves in a time in which the whole of existence on this planet is taking an evolutionary step.

So what is happening in this evolutionary step? You should recognize that all the earthly ways of looking at things that you had up to now only present one side of the whole. Learning, that means to develop through evolution, now has an entirely new importance and another meaning from before. **Learning is now becoming a memory**, but not an earthly memory, but rather a Divine Memory. The Divine Memory encompasses everything. Within the Divine Memory, everything is contained. Within the Divine Memory your physical memories are transformed, and in that way all suffering is released, as suffering only exists in your physical memory. This evolutionary step makes it possible for you to live a life in Divine Consciousness. This is the consciousness that you normally experience only after your death, when you go into the Light. That is also the Light from which you come when you are born, and die into this world.

All are helping to lift the consciousness here on the Earth up to the Divine Consciousness. Perhaps you believe that many are working against this and want to prevent it. We tell you, however, that everything here is going according to plan, as those who are defending themselves rigidly against their consciousness of freedom, and fight for this point of view, as was once the task of all of you, are merely condensing their human energy field in order to burst open this hard shell of theirs. Did you know that the earthly consciousness of these people is not aware of any other way out of this great feeling of self-contempt? This is one of the many ways to take leave of the Earth. Which way will you choose? How will you meet your beautiful star light that is beginning to shine more and more in you, and causing everything that would hinder this light to simply dissolve away? Will you allow yourself to be enchanted by the light, or allow yourself to be frightened by the melting process?

Of course, you will allow yourself to be enchanted—be good to yourself! Then you will always find the right, light-filled way that shows you the path and the destination through all earthly turbulence.

For you are the destination—your Star Light!

All of this is a Divine Thought. Just as you are living out your task here on the Earth in a more and more conscious way, every being that does service on, in, or in the vicinity of the planet, has its task to fulfill. Think about it: judgment and condemnation are tools of the earthly dimension! When you criticize yourself for your own judgments and condemnation, once again you only see from an earthly perspective. Just put everything to one side! Just leave everything in peace! Just let everything simply BE! Look at yourself from the perspective of the stars!

Why is all this happening, you perhaps ask yourself? As you surely know, the earthly sense of time has to do with vibration. Think of this as a wave. At some point in time and in some way, this wave was set in motion, and during all this time the Earth has been subject to various forces within the movements of this wave. Yes, the Earth itself sailed along on this wave, and just like this wave, on the Earth the forces of the Cosmos could be perceived as being at a particular height, strength, and density. It is still that way now. Now you have reached the crest of this wave. Yes, that's how tall the wave has become! Now is a time of liberation! Now you can immediately see what you create, what you wish for.

It is your deepest wish for security, comfort, and warmth that now once again makes your whole spectrum of wishes visible. All these idealized images pass in front of you. In the process you decide what you consider to be of value, and you give form to this. Thus, if the ideal of beauty strikes a chord in your being then it will endure here on the Earth, as these are the new building blocks upon which and by means of which things will be built on the Earth. On the other hand, if your values detector comes to rest in front of another picture that does not correspond to your true self-image and your true greatness but rather to an old memory of a tiny cage, in which you were locked up, you also bring this to expression, and in that way this cage can also simply melt away, at some point.

It is so easy! Just be aware that you are a thought of God. What could ever be wrong with Him? Free yourself from your old memory by taking the lid away from the limitation. Imagine that all the beauty that you always projected onto God, onto the angels, and into Heaven is waiting for you. Where? Here! **Because you are this beauty!** Yes, that is how it is!

All your feelings and views are relative. You are free due to your innermost light. Let it shine in this world! You are so valuable and in the right place, here on the Earth. Every being that hides its light under a bushel feels drawn to your light. You recognize one another in the light.

It is good that we may tell you again that you are nothing other than the Light of God. You are a valiant worker here on the Earth. You do your service and allow yourself to be guided by your true beauty. You are all such beautiful beings! This is a special Festival of Joy — this is your return home, this is your evolutionary step. Be who you are! This is you. You are Divine Love that is vibrating.

We love you and hold your hands in ours. We are at your side and give you courage. Thus you are full of delight, in your human existence. We love you!

Your Star Friends, your Star Children

Time

Hello, Beloved! We are always there. We are always at your side, even when you are working hard and struggling—we are always there. We exist always in Love, in joy, in delight. You might call our state one of ease. Were you always in a state of ease yourself lately? We waited for you seventeen times. It is nice that you are with us once again. In what way are you with us? In the ease of your Soul and your Spirit!

For your Spirit, your true nature, there is no brooding over things. Your Spirit develops in a very particular manner of experiencing things. Between your Spirit, your Soul, and your earthly way of thinking there is a highly unusual communication at work. In order to bring this process a little closer to you, we request once again that you look at yourself not only from the human vantage point but also from the level of experience of your Soul and from the state of unconditional Love of your Spirit.

]Your Spirit is contented and happy. Your Spirit is rest and activity at the same time. For your Spirit, everything is possible! Your Spirit vibrates in a very particular way. It can go everywhere. Your Spirit is YOU. Your soul is already an expression of your Spirit. Your Soul is a form of energy that is already familiar with the difference between giving and taking. One might also say it like this: your Soul is a form of energy which links being and becoming, giving and taking, and so with the components of time. This characterizes your earthly consciousness particularly strongly. **Here in this illusion you experience everything that exists "at the same time", as one thing after another.** You are pure Spirit—you are thus pure being that is EVERYTHING that exists. Thus you are an individual expression of this being which simply conforms to temporal aspects. By this means all forms of illusion arise, which you as human beings are familiar with here. In this way you experience the Existence of Everything as though it takes place one thing after another. And nevertheless, everything is the same. It is an experience of the various aspects of time within the ONE. Yes, that is you. You are a part of this beauty that opens up within time.

**We want to tell you about the Love within time,
for time is also Love.**

You can form your own experience of time. Can you remember how you experienced time as a child? Compare this with how you now, as an adult, experience time. As a child you were still so connected to the temporal quality of your Soul and your Spirit. For that reason this denser experience of time on the Earth seems to you to have lasted so long. You could describe the experience of time as the Cross that you carry here on the Earth. Or, let's say: **experiencing time in your earthly consciousness, compared to the experience of time in your Soul and Spirit consciousness, is like a heavy cross resting on your shoulders.** Haven't YOU spoken so often of a cross? Of course, you don't have to carry this cross! You will put it down when you recognize in every moment the illusion of time—then you accept time's Love. In that way it becomes relative for you, once again, and is released. Time is your instrument of experience here on the Earth.

On your journey home you decide how much time you spend on your memories and how much Love you allot to time—how much Love you give yourself from time, as time is not given to you so that you suffer but rather that you recognize God within it. God? Might we mean with that the Source of Love? Might we mean you? Bull's eye!

**Time is a vehicle by means of which you find and
recognize yourself again.**

Time is a holy instrument. If you allow yourself to be endowed by its Love, then it dissolves and you are once again whole and experience unity with your Soul and Spirit.

You can imagine this like riding a bicycle. You ride your bike, starting from your center, from your Existence of All, from your Spirit, and the further you go the more intense is your experience of time. The further you ride your bicycle away from the center, in which everything exists at the same time, the more you experience this whole as something happening next to and after one another. The further out you travel with your bicycle the more slowly you will experience time to be, just as you would as though everything were moving in slow motion. Go even further, until you experience the distances and time itself even more intensely, until they seem to be standing still. **By the way, the bicycle you are riding is your Soul.** You can remember the Universal Consciousness at every point, at every place along your bicycle tour. This is possible at every point! Why? Because the Source is not something separate from you. You are the Source that is exploring itself with this special adventure on your bicycle.

This exploration is the kind of experience that the Source picks up on "away" from the Center. In the midst of the Universal Consciousness, no exploration is necessary. We know how paradoxical this must sound from the human point of view. Let time dissolve away for a short period of time. Get down from your bike for just a short moment and cancel time. How? **With Love!**

We continue to wish you a good trip on your adventure! Perhaps it will become easier and easier for you to recognize the essence of being in everything that you come across on your journey? Perhaps the idea that you are at home no matter where you go with your bicycle, will become more and more a reality? Perhaps the idea that you are already at home appeals to you?

We will continue to wait for you until you have understood the Love that is in time within your heart. Then you can go everywhere and be everywhere at the same time, be everything and also nothing at the same time.

We love you, you courageous cyclist and explorer. You are the beauty of the Cosmos! In you is reflected all that exists! Be gentle towards your human existence!

We love you!

    The Star Children

Polarity — Love

Once again we have a message for you. We wish to tell you how much we love you and that it is possible for you as a human being to feel yourself within the unity, the warmth, the comfort of the Source. Have you ever felt "lost"? Have you ever had the feeling that you had lost the connection to the Source and to other people? Have you ever felt truly alone, in this way? Do you know that this is a state of mind that you can only experience as a human being?

This is a state of intense illusion in which you believe that you and Love exist separately from one another. Seen from our vantage point and from your plane of Love this kind of perception is truly a phenomenon. In order to be able to even experience this state of illusion and to consider it to be valid, you have to take on for example the form of human existence. Now this doesn't mean that earthly existence in this form represents your true human existence. No! Otherwise you might believe yourself to be truly lost, here on the Earth! No! Human existence is something quite beautiful, and today we even tell you: in this regard, human existence is something quite special! **As a human being you can even experience Love as a kind of polarity!** In the Cosmos there are a number of beings and places which are right now also undergoing the experience of being separated and of a lack of Love in their consciousness. The task of these beings is to go through this phase of consciousness. That which sets you human beings apart is the ability to be aware at every moment, at all times, of your cosmic origins and your cosmic Love, that is, of your divinity!

You as human beings are a species that can experience both poles, namely Love and the illusion of being separated from Love. This is what is meant by experiencing Love as a polarity. Yes, now, at this moment, you can be aware of the divine nature of yourself and of others, as well as that of every creature on your planet. But—you also possess in equal measure the ability to give yourself up to the illusion of being at a distance from it as well. This is the special aspect of human existence. Perhaps you believed at one time that you had to be or do something special in order to achieve divinity. It is actually the opposite of that. The special aspect of human existence is the fact that you can experience within your consciousness the apparent absence of your true nature. There, on the plane where you find yourself by means of the experience of the illusion that you are cut off from the creative Divine Source, you have the opportunity to bring your radiant light, to awaken. That is something truly great that you are capable of as a human being!

There are times in your human existence in which you have concentrated on living separately. Now your focus is once again turning to the opposite of this. Now you are experiencing the reconnection, the unification of your true self with the Love that you are. You have explored and fulfilled many tasks and missions on the plane of living in separation. Now you are here so that you can kindle the Light on all the planes that you have experienced as polarity. By means of your dedication, the realm of consciousness and awareness of unconditional Love is expanding. By means of that which you do and you experience, you broaden the expanse of the consciousness of Love. Imagine the Source of Love as a sphere with a glowing center. From this center, Love radiates outward. As a human being you have so often experienced yourself as being at the edge of this sphere, far away from the Source. We say to you: by means of your experience you enlarge the center of the Source so that it reaches you where you are as a human being. This is your light-filled service!

How often do you think you act out of ignorance? How often, as we said at the beginning, do you feel yourself to be lost and think that you only do wrong? Hand over all these apparent inadequacies to your deepest inner Source—that is God. This Source provided all of this that you do and experience here, with great, very great, Love. Yes, this Source is you! If it's easier to accept this, you can describe this Source as the deepest part of you. In truth, you are it in its entirety. WE want to help you to let go of the conviction that you are something unworthy, as: **if you consider yourself, or some part of you, to be unworthy, then you create this as something that you will be able to illuminate with the Light of Love at a later point in time.** This is the eternal cycle of Love and its polarity that you can experience.

You are all such important workers here on this planet. It was not beneath you to come here. For that reason you are esteemed!

You came here because you knew that you can accomplish everything that you have to do. Nothing is impossible for you if you look at it from your Soul and Spirit connection, as you are the being that has entered into the experience of polarity and can experience at the same time the oneness of all existence—a singular polarity. We stand in such a humble attitude before you, for that which you do. We thank you, you "secret" Master!

Now you no longer need to conceal your mastery.
This is the good news which you as a being of unconditional Love have been authorized to bring to yourself as a human being.

We love you! Thank you for your service! Thank you for taking on and experiencing all the polarizing perspectives, while you always knew inside that you are a part of the whole. We love you just the way you are. Do you love yourself just the way you are?

In radiant joy, in deep humility!

>   Your Star Children, your Star Friends

A Walk

Beloved Earth Dwellers, we are always with you. It doesn't matter how you feel, we are always with you. We would like to talk to you today about your human life—about that which you create and experience there. Now you might ask, "Does that mean that I create everything for myself—including my unhappiness, apathy, or discouragement?"

Well, Beloved Child, we have it easy. We can look at you and everything that happens to you from our vantage point. This is the point of view and the state of LOVE. Even if you human beings seem to move away from this Love, this always happens with only a part of your consciousness. You cannot ever move entirely away from Love, as it is Love that brings you all the experiences that you want to have. If you are depressed, unhappy, or discouraged, if you can no longer find any meaning in life, and if inner struggles take place within you, then this always happens in only one part of your consciousness. Your Love, that is, your entire being—your true, real being—remains unaffected by this.

You come to this planet in order to experience, to undergo Love in a quite special way. **You might say that you are testing Love to see to what extent it is capable of giving you everything that you wish for.** Once again, this sounds like a paradox, doesn't it? Perhaps it is you yourself whom you are testing, to see how far Love determines your actions. This is one of the special privileges you humans have. What sort of privileges are those, anyway—what does that mean? This might be your next question. So, what is meant by these privileges? You can understand this most readily if you simply see things as they are:

**You have come to this planet in order to
experience your ability to Love, here on the Earth.
The only thing you have to do for this is:
LIVE—live your earthly life.**

We would like to illustrate this for you by means of an example. Imagine that you go for a walk along the same path every day. You already know this path inside and out. You know where it starts and where it ends. You have gone this way so often that one day you decide to do the following: **Now I will walk this path blindfolded!** I want to see what this path is like if I don't use my eyes, but rather other means of perception, as a compass!

Do you know what we mean? Your life on Earth is like this walk with blindfolded eyes, as now you set off on your walk and come across everything to be found there using another kind of perception. Now it might happen that you suddenly experience an "object" on your path as a threat. Why did this happen? Because you did not trust yourself to walk straight ahead the way you are used to doing on your walk. You actually went a little to one side and ran into an obstacle. Well, you can recall right away what this obstacle is, how familiar it is, and that you don't need to be afraid of it. Grasp it, feel its shape, and you will recognize it for what it is! It was always there along your path. Now you can set off calmly again and continue your journey with your eyes blindfolded until you reach your goal. What is the goal? To go your way in complete confidence! You know that! Don't let yourself be intimidated! If you come across something once more that makes you afraid, just stop for a little while and remind yourself what the path looked like when you followed it all those times with your eyes open. Remind yourself what it is that you are meeting at that moment, as you always went along your way before this in peace and confidence. Doesn't that sound easy? We tell you that it is exactly like that!

Your earthly life is like a walk during which you test yourself by taking it with your eyes blindfolded. We would like to tell you that you wouldn't do this if you didn't know the path in its entirety beforehand. In your earthly life you only follow paths that you have already checked out in your other dimension as a spiritual being. You have walked them so often until you decided to take your final exam here on the Earth and to walk this path blindfolded.

We love you! Everything that you do here changes the vibration on this planet. This so-called examination is an act of Love which you have decided to take for your sake and for that of Mother Earth. We thank you for that which you do here! We thank you for your earthly journey. Whenever you wish for help then just sense that we are holding your hand. Rely on it! We are together with you in such Love. This is the Love in which you have come here, the Love in which you made your decision to go your way here. We love you just the way you are! We love you for that which you are! We all do the same work. We all perform the same service—each in his particular domain. We know that you go your way in confidence, and that it doesn't matter to you if you walk with your eyes open or closed, as under your feet you sense Mother Earth, who carries you on this journey. Through the air that you breathe you experience the limitless Divine Universal Power which walks on this path. By means of your hands and your heart you can recognize everything that has been made available for your use on your earthly path. Everything that comes to meet you on this path is ready to open its arms to you and shake your hand in order to congratulate you that you have come so far on your journey.

We love you! We admire you and thank you! Keep in mind: the tighter your blindfold feels to you, that much more confidence and Love you possess, which can open up and blossom!

In Love

    Your guides, the Star Children

Self-esteem — Consciousness — Love

Hello, Beloved, dear and valued friend! We wait for you again and again because we have so much Love for you—so much Love.

What do you actually think you are worth? We are asking you this question as it is a very important one. It is geared towards your consciousness. How much are you worth, and what is "worth" anyway? **As valuable as you are to yourself, that is how much God is worth to you. As much Love as you can feel for God, that is how much Love you can feel for yourself.** So just reflect on it: how much is God worth to you? How much are you worth to yourself?

What happens if you continue to neglect your self-esteem, now and again? What actually happens if you lose the deep, sincere love, the high opinion, and the respect you feel for yourself? Do you think it is still possible to truly love God? Look at the whole thing from the other side and consider with what immeasurable Love God loves all human beings? Do you think that God could do this if He didn't also love Himself in the same way? "Yes, this is easy for God, he is Love," you might now say. Do you think you are any different? If yes, then be careful, as then this is namely the form that your consciousness assumes, that is you. As you perceive yourself, the way that you think about yourself and the feelings that arise in regard to this, what opinion you hold in regard to yourself—that is all a part of that which manifests itself through you and in you.

This is a part of the earthly game that you play here. Among other things, you exchange opinions about who and what you are, and these identifications are what make up your identity. For that reason consider well which convictions and opinions from other people you accept as your own! Over time they will become those that you live out, in the end, and that you are. Would you like to BE that which another person represents as a personal view of the world? Weigh up, precisely and with clarity, whether such convictions correspond to your deepest and truest being. Discover your own true being and everything that characterizes it. The next time you exchange opinions, convictions, and energies with someone else, observe how quickly these can manifest themselves and become your own identity.

Who are you in reality? You are a being that here on the earth is capable of an intense exchange of energy with everything that comes to meet you. You can limit yourself completely by means of your identification and seemingly distance yourself from the Source. But you can also allow yourself and your identity to merge with the Source completely. In this state you will experience what Love the Source has for you and within what Love you truly exist in the Cosmos. **Your tool to discovering this is consciousness.** We encourage you to work with this tool and to act and exist within its limitless power, as everything that the Source is, is also you—and you are everything that the Source is.

All the Love, power, and devotion of the Source are available for your use so that they can be experienced on this planet. This consciousness automatically motivates other forms of energy to achieve the same level of perception. Thus it is also the same with other states of consciousness that you experience. Becoming aware of yourself and the world is always an invitation to other forms of consciousness and energy. For that reason you find yourself again in the world that you believe in. All the power lies in your consciousness. **This power is nothing else but Love.** This power is an appropriate description of your true nature. You can easily take leave of your inner convictions about your earthly self-image and your self-definition. How? Through the power of Love within your consciousness. Look at this power as a present that God has given you. At every moment of your life, this present sits there before you. When are you going to open it? Why don't you open it right away, and experience how good you actually feel within yourself and how beautiful you actually are? God gives you this gift in every moment anew. That is unconditional Love. You can appreciate what you do with it by seeing how much Love you allow for yourself—how much Love you allow for God.

\It is so nice to see your anticipation at opening this present. Unpack it! You can hardly imagine how much Love you are, in reality. If you accept that then you also pass this Love onto those around you; then you make them an invitation, so to speak. Today we have come to you in the form of this present. Thank you that you opened it and perceived us within it! We love you! We love you immeasurably. We love you the way you are and for that which you are! For we know that your Love is nothing else but the Love of God.

Greetings—your friends in the consciousness of Love!

    Your friends, the Star Children

Inner Space

Hello, Beloved. We are always with you. Yes, we are always with you. We are always particularly close when YOU allow yourself to be touched by our vibration of Love. For many of you it is easier to think that these vibrations of Love come to you from the outside. Many are of the opinion that they take hold of you and that you are connected with them in that way. In truth it is exactly the opposite of this, as these vibrations of Love are you—they are not something separate from you. They are your true nature.

When you wake up in the morning and return from your nightly astral journeys and other trips within your earthly consciousness your Soul is often in a state of great bliss. Then you remember as much of the Love you experienced as you are capable of experiencing with your earthly consciousness. Every one of you experiences leaving the body in sleep in a different way. When you leave your body and are in addition free of fear, your consciousness journeys to a beautiful plane of ease and lightness and experiences this as a kind of rejuvenation. Now we ask you why this kind of experience is not possible also during the daytime? We tell you that it is possible! How?

Just follow your inner space, your inner quiet, your inner Love, your inner power, and you will reach the center of existence.

This will help you to experience more and more often and more and more easily who and what you in truth are. By this means you can practically discover whether you are merely the consciousness that you experience on the Earth through your identification, or whether the limitless Source of All Existence is manifest in you.

This discovery can be a lot of fun for you human beings. In the process it can happen that you are torn back and forth between your various possibilities of perception. On the one hand there is the human, earthly perception. It tells you who you are as a person and how you experience the world. And "behind it", there is this other perception. Give yourself over to the lightness of your being while you explore these various levels of perception. By the way—earthly perception and forms of consciousness are quite prepared to defend their identities.

Thus as a human being you are capable of various states of consciousness and experience. Why should you not have the right to decide for the one or the other, one in which everything finds room and love and above all, security? Your earthly consciousness possesses above all a demand for security. Only, how reliable is your earthly perception? Isn't that an amusing contradiction in itself? Aren't you already chuckling a little over this contradiction? How secure can it be for the Universal Spirit to experience itself in a human and "limited" body? Just as securely as the extent to which you permit this limitless Spirit to express and realize itself in and above your earthly existence.

If you make use of your boundless potential, then you have so very much at your disposal! Here in this dimension there are no limitations. And within your capacity to love you also have so much to draw on. What should hinder you, in truth, from drawing constantly on this reservoir? In this state of consciousness, you can experience in your daily life your true nature of existence more and more fully. Thus in every moment you can enjoy the highest measure of Love and security. **You are everything that you need for this—you as Soul and you as Spirit, you as God.** The nice thing about this is that in this way you can enjoy the earthly game more and more; it is for this game, for this limitless experience, that you came here. It is you who makes Love a reality! Be aware of this!

We are with you with as much Love and joy as you allow. Imagine now how great this can be if you allow there to be more and more Love and trust. Isn't that a nice way to grow as a human being into All-Embracing Love? One thought, one moment are enough, and you are here on the Earth in the true nature of your existence.

We love you so much. We value you and respect every decision you make regarding the configuration of your earthly life. It is you who are turning history around on the planet. Your Love lies in the hands of God. That is the true nature of your existence. Be happy about who you really are!

Your loving friends, your Star Children

Spark

Beloved Earth Friend!

Do you long for "spiritual guidance"—for someone who can give you loving advice in every situation? If you like, you can call us that, as in a certain way we are also your loving spiritual leader. This is what we are for all of those who wish for this kind of connection. Otherwise we simply remain always connected to you with our loving energy. We appear to you in the way that you wish to see us. If you want to paint us dark grey, then this is a reflection of your thoughts. Now you will probably ask yourself what is meant by this dark grey color?

This is what is meant: all the Love that we have for you shines upon you like a sun. This Love flows through you and radiates into your entire being. There where you yourself have placed barriers and limits instead of Love, this light cannot radiate into these areas in you, because they throw shadows. That is how simple it is. Perhaps you can better understand by means of this how it is that a number of people have constructed so many constraints and limitations instead of Love. They cannot see this bright, radiant, and warm light any more. Those who can still perceive the light but see strong projections of shadows consider them to be energy that comes to them from "above," or from outside themselves.

Beloved! We say this to you: you have come here in bright, radiant light and have created various shadows in earthly life through your consciousness. Yes, you did that consciously by placing your faith in various other energies instead of in your true nature, and made them your own. Thus you have made a landmark out of a small pebble in your great mosaic of light. This light-shielding boulder appears to you to be more appropriate here on the Earth than your radiant mosaic of light.

With your consciousness, by means of your will and your deliberation, you can ally yourself with various qualities of energy. If you connect yourself to outward-flowing and expansive Love, this has the effect of an initial spark, like a spark that sets a fire alight or a substance that sets off a reaction. Thus you are a positive, nurturing aspect within the flowing process of creation in the Cosmos. If you ally yourselves with a stagnant or destructive energy then this is the opposite of the process of creation. Then you take on the form of a shadow. As a result what you see of the light of creation and the energy of creation are the shadows that are reflected. Usually you interpret this then as negative energy from without that hinders you unjustly in your life.

Today our message for you sounds like this: **Let yourself be set on fire by the spark of the energy of creation!** Allow yourself to be touched by this energy! In that way you can transform all your human protective mechanisms, those which are meant to protect you against your own power, back into Love once again. The Cosmos finds itself in constant growth, that is, in a constant process of creation. Creation is a conscious form of energy that is expanding. That is what you call it in your three-dimensional world, at least.

You are the creators on this Earth! You are constantly changing this place! Just let the light of the Cosmos, the creative force of the All-Loving Source pulsate within you once more. Yes, you can do it!

For you human beings creation means constantly breaking through the barriers of thought until you pass over into the condition of the existence of everything.

Your world is built on thoughts. It forms itself out of your wishes and your desires and is subject to a very rapid transformation. The Spirit in its existence knows continuity, however. Whenever you allow yourself to fall into the Oneness of the Spirit then this can shake your thought structure like an earthquake. This is then a thought-quake. You often experience this then as a personal crisis. You are the channel, the intermediary of the transition from All-Existing Love onto the human plane of earthly existence. Here on the Earth you are both. Isn't that wonderful? This is like a connecting tube out of whose earthly opening streams perpetual Love. That is you! You can therefore allow yourself to be guided by your Spirit and your Soul without needing earthly thoughts as well. Aren't you then in that case your own "spiritual guide?"

We tell you, however, that nevertheless your thoughts are a form of earthly energy of creation. If you want to give form to an intention, to shape energy, begin with a thought. Let it stream from your heart with Love and you will reap a rich harvest, as you human beings are wont to say. That is an act of creation!

Where does this creative energy come from? From yourself, from the deepest part of you! You are a channel. You are this transition where identity arises from out of All-Existing Love. Thus, you came to Earth—as an infant, free of identity, connected only to the loving Creative Force, but becoming more and more the being that you are in your physical body. **Turn this body and your world into your Heaven!** That is the term that you have always used for your connection to your spiritual home, for the other end of this connecting tube.

Do you see how powerful you are? Do you see how creation works? Love is a power that gives itself and does not limit itself! Isn't that a beautiful kind of devotion? This devotion is your energy potential!

Be Love, and then you have everything you wish for! Then you can say, "The Spirit of God is among us," as it is Love.

We value your work, your service on the Earth. You are a creative force, you are a creative will—now, at this moment. All the Love that you need and that you wish for is given to you. Thank you for your courageous service! Your spiritual connection of Love knows very well what you do here. Thank you that you as a human being are transforming yourself into this loving being!

Your spiritual friends,
Your loving advisors

    The Star Children

Power Station

We greet you, our dear, curious recipient of our message! Do you sometimes ask yourself how your life will move forward—whether you will finally listen to your inner voice and trust it, or continue to obey your little fears and worries?

You human beings are light! Now you raise an objection here: "But I learned that we are light and shadow, here on the Earth?" Our answer is as follows: Yes and no! Yes, because here on the Earth you allow yourselves to be impressed by reflections and projections, and no, because your true being is the projector. It is all about light.

Yes, you are light! How do you like the idea that all of you bring light to the Earth yourselves? You ask yourselves so often, "Why am I here?" Your earthly consciousness poses this question. When you become aware of your origins, if you discover them, you will realize WHY you are here. After that you will ask yourself HOW you should accomplish this? Then we will show you your light.

And now life will become a great joy, as all the light that you need and wish for comes from within yourself.

You can imagine it like this: within you there is a secret generator, a secret power station that can produce endless power, Love, and success. This power station transforms your spiritual Soul Light into earthly Love—into light. When you get this power station going, first you will illuminate your own personality, the layers of your human consciousness, with this radiant energy of success. By doing so you will see everything that is hindering you in this process. Meet all of that with determined

Love and clarity! And when you have removed your own hindrances, your power station will radiate and emit so much happiness, peace of mind, and joy that everything you think about becomes Love. This power is within you! All right, how do you get this power station started? Where is the "on" button here? **It is within your heart.** Whenever you feel warmth, confidence, and certainty as well as devotion, then this power station is in operation. When all of your feelings of guilt related to your being here on the Earth have dissolved, then nothing can hold you back. Then you are one of these Divine Power Stations here on the Earth. Of course you are this power station from the start, as soon as you arrive here. You only need to find the switch.

You should be aware of just how much the energy of guilt can hold you back from your own energy. That is how easy it can be. What you call enlightenment, wisdom, or the path of enlightenment we call today: **your power station.** If it has gone on line and is working at capacity then you are "enlightened." Then you exist in the light—the Light of your Soul, of the Spirit, of the Source.

What do you think? When is the right moment to get this power station up and running? Tomorrow? Have you noticed that you just turned it on? Layer for layer, you accept this Love and power and trust that you are. With it you overcome one obstacle after another in order to truly enjoy the service provided by the power station, as you have come into the world so as to have joy in life! Joy—that is your light, your power. How do you like this feeling, this clarity? Everything that you do takes place within the light of your spiritual home and your spiritual companions, because you have not come here alone to do your work. All of you work on raising the vibration on the Earth with the support of your power stations. Mother Earth is also helping you out. She knows who you are and is aware of your missions. You can sense her in Love and perceive your mutual trust and cooperation with one another.

Your light is a divine light. Live within it and relish it! Within this light and this joy, there we are too—and we always meet one another there! We thank you, stand by your side, and support you, you beautiful Child of Man!

We love you!

    The Star Children

Self-Love

We love you, you wonderful creature of God! Today we wish to ask you, dear Earth Dweller, if you sometimes feel exhausted? We assure you that you will be rewarded for your work and for all the effort that you expend here on the Earth! Sounds pretty good, doesn't it?

Our Beloved! We would like to remind you that you are the countenance of God. **The countenance of God**—whatever can that mean? That means that God loves you as you are! You yourself always only like yourself if your self-perception is accompanied by certain emotions. Yes, you like yourself really only then, when you are experiencing conditions that are pleasant physically and emotionally. If you live through phases in which life is a little more difficult, and you don't feel well within yourself at every moment, then you don't like yourself—then you reject yourself. But you really aren't being very nice to yourself!

We suggest that you should like yourself even if you don't feel well and happy. Often you don't feel so well within yourself because your behavior, or the behavior of your surroundings, doesn't correspond to your preconceived ideas. Another time, you are uncomfortable, and you don't know at all why. What is going on with you? We would like to explain this to you and to present a possible solution.

Imagine what would happen if God were dissatisfied with us. Do you think something like that exists? In the divine power of creation, in which God exists and "manifests" Himself, the whole of existence would instantly become dissatisfaction itself. Wouldn't that be rather fatal? What do you think? And YOU are also a creator working in many dimensions. We already spoke about the ways that you can deal with painful emotional states without handing them the reins. It is important that you pay attention to the following: it is up to you what energies, thoughts, and emotions you create and how you react to the selfsame when they come to meet you. **Everything that meets you gives you the possibility of dealing with it.**

Yes, it is God who places this whole game of life at your disposal, so that you can grow and learn from it. Your studies take place in the spiritual dimension. You would call it the heavenly Plane of Love. And **growth** takes place here on the Earth. Here on the Earth you grow into all of that which you prepared for and studied for on your spiritual, heavenly plane. Yes, you want to fulfill all of that here and nothing more! For that reason we wish to encourage you to listen to your inner voice, your inner space, and your Love. Isn't all of that already familiar to you? It is certainly nothing new for you anymore. The Love that you wish for from us and from all your spiritual companions is something that you actually possess.

You only need to act from out of the deepest part of yourself and then you act out of Love.

In the earthly dimension there are many different forms of consciousness. You human beings are a special case as you are capable of being conscious of your creative force and your origin. **You can get in touch with your Source and become it, here on the Earth**. Isn't that a great joy? Isn't that enough motivation to do this?

You are not alone here, but are rather a little mosaic tile in the great Divine Picture. All the tiles together make up this wonderful picture of creation. Look at this picture now from a distance. Can you see how important the little tile is that you are? Can you see how important every tile is? Yes, every little tile is important! You can choose the color of this little tile embedded in the whole. Can you see how colorful the whole picture is? All the tiles receive their light and their color from the middle, from their center. Who gives them this color there? Who gives you this color there? Is it perhaps YOU?

We love you the way you are! And we know that you can understand that in a different way from before. Let yourself be embraced! Your friends, the Star Children, present you with their Love and esteem, their complete faith in you. We are holding your hand and giving you a big hug, as we were always the most loving and the best of friends. We love you! We give you our joy. We are so happy that you are our beloved friend. We love you!

Your Star Friends, the Star Children

Contrasts

Beloved!

We know how intensely you are searching for the light at this time. We are familiar with your pain and for your motivation for this. We would like to tell you that we are accompanying your search. Yes! In times of Love it is easy for you to comprehend this. We assure you however of our constant presence!

You are a Child of God! Is this something you can experience within yourself—that every creature is a Child of God? This is something that is perhaps difficult for you to perceive if you look at all the contrasting opinions, convictions, and views of others. Isn't it sometimes difficult to believe, and very surprising as well, that all earthly, controversial views should be equally valid? If you find yourself for example in a situation of conflict, it probably sounds contentious that all those involved in it are equal in value to one another? This point of view may represent a particular challenge for you, but just open yourself up to it! Yes!

> **The real challenge here on the Earth is BEAUTY,
> to take joy in the beauty of existence.**

If you can see the beauty of your surroundings then you can also see your own beauty. It you can find joy in your surroundings beyond your I centered consciousness, then you can also find joy in regard to yourself. All you need for it are your own eyes. We are speaking here of your Eyes of the Soul. We have already shown them to you. Use the Eyes of the Soul, and you can see everything from the point of view of the community, the communality of all your earthly service in all that takes place on the planet!

Sometimes it is just easier to trust in the higher connections between things. This is quite right! From within the Love out of which you came here, every other being has also come here. Every single earthly being is important to God. That is unconditional Love. You can look at your knowledge and actions from the point of view that it exists not merely for itself but is there for everyone. What would it mean to you on its own? Could you fulfill your Love, in that case? Every living being, every human being on the Earth carries the determination within it to be part of the whole and to represent a part of the whole on the Earth.

We love you! It is getting easier and easier for you to recognize your Love and to give it as well. No one is alone on this planet. No one has come merely for himself alone. No one lives for himself alone. You and everything you know are LOVE, even if you perhaps aren't that happy as a human being to hear that. Your Soul is working on putting this into action, and your Spirit is accomplishing all of this. Unconditional Love is streaming from the Source of Love. It is up to you how much you want to accept this, as the more you are aware of this and can accept it, the more you as a human being will become this Source and your true existence. Thus you attain your own existence.

We invite you to experience the unconditional Love, the complete acceptance of existence, your own existence—perfect Cosmic Love. At times you can already perceive its rays from afar. Then it is very easy for you to experience it. At other times, you still don't really believe in it, even if it is looking you straight in the eye. Everything that exists carries the beauty of the Source within it. This is something quite natural for your Spirit. This can be motivation enough for your Soul to come here to the Earth, so that it can implement it here. As a human being you are often amazed at what you are capable of. Keep on being amazed, that's fine!

Remember that your Love is everything that you have to give. It is common property! Is it easy for you to think this way? Just imagine that God would keep His Love all to himself. Would you like that? Every human being is free to take advantage of the opportunity to be touched by this Love and to transform all the heaviness of life into lightness. Your service here on the Earth goes far beyond human calculation. You all do much more than you can recognize, as human beings. Your limitless

Love makes it all possible for you! What should be denied you, or be impossible for you? Yes, everything on this Earth that you let yourself be truly impressed by, or fascinated by, is unconditional and limitless Love.

We leave you there within your all-powerful Love. That is true omnipotence! That is true power—it is yours! Live it out!

We love you, Child of Man! Do you still feel yourself in need of anything? We present you with our Love and our esteem for your tireless search. We admire your energy. It is your Love that the Earth needs. **It is your Love that beautifies life on Earth.** If you could see your true nature of Love for just an instant you would wait upon yourself and greet yourself with the same compliments and the same esteem. We thank you for your earthly service! Thank you for your existence and for your work! Thank you for your Love! You are no abstract, ineffectual being on the Earth. It is you that Creation is counting on!

    Your friends in Love, the Star Children

Divine Motivation

We greet you, our dear and valued friend!

You ask if there is a message for you, for all of you? Yes, there is always a message for you. You only need to listen deep within yourself, to listen to your inner voice. You human beings live in a very loud world. For that reason it is perhaps a challenge to hear the right one among all those voices—to identify the Divine Voice. Do you think you could identify it if you weren't divine yourself? Listen to yourself, for God speaks from within you! Once again this may perhaps sound spooky or implausible to a number of you.

We will continue to remind you, over and over again, just how valuable your existence is.

Sometimes you lose sight of the meaning of life and the joy of life because you have no idea anymore how valuable you are to the Cosmos. You might even call this a "side-effect of your Incarnation," or the price you have to pay for it.

As soon as you allow yourself to feel your own value for even a moment, you already exist within your divine perception. Yes, it is enough if you give yourself up to it for a moment and perceive your worth! Everything that God gives you is His. Thus Love flows from the powerful, divine dimension into your heart, and you can say, "This Love is mine!" Love is a gift that you can give to yourself. God is the All-Embracing Love that takes care of everything. In essence there is no difference between the Love that you receive here in life and that which you give here, on the Earth. The power of God is in your midst! If you bring together in lightness all the experiences that you have had on the Earth, it is God who stands before you and invites you to a life lived with joy.

We love you, our friend, and we see what a remarkable point on your journey you have already reached.

> **You can do something very positive if for a moment you put aside your illusory thoughts and accept that your life is determined by divine motivation.**

You come to the Earth to do the crazy things that you consider so important. You consider that which so many strive for, which other people do, to be mad, or you consider your own activities to be mad. We say to you: all of your actions are motivated by Divine Power! You couldn't even create your crazy life situations if God did not provide you with them. Do you see how much creative energy there is in you? Now it only remains for you to employ it for your own enjoyment and for the enjoyment of others, as then you can, all of you can, survive all your dark times, or in other words, illuminate them! Then you will feel equal to all your challenges.

Sometimes the Divine Plan appears to be baffling. **Don't try to understand it, but rather to live it!** Many human Souls on the Earth are approaching a point at which they are confronting their fears. Being able to accept your worth and enjoy a meaningful life of joy means that you let go of your fear of it, as you have all brought your own salvation with you to the Earth. Every person put a piece of it in his bag, as food for the journey, before coming to the Earth. Every person received so much that by means of it he is a radiant, shining light on the Earth. Well, then—the more human beings allow themselves to shine in this light and to be so full of light themselves, that much earlier will the sleep of ignorance and lack of awareness vanish from the planet. Just imagine it like this: God comes to stand before you. Do you think that He would punish you? Or do you think that you would recognize your true home, in God? Then you would recognize everything that represents Love and happiness for you to be something self-evident, and in that moment you would create it by this means within your Divine Power.

**What you believe in and what seems important to you,
is what you create!**

Seize the right for yourself to gaze at your radiant light! In that way, you lose all fear of yourselves. In that way, life loses the weight of loneliness. By means of your light-filled presence, you emit this energy and are for many what they call God. Yes, you are the bringers of light on this Earth. You are remembering this more and more readily, and more and more often. In this way, however, you are not alienated from human existence. Quite the contrary! You will make manifest here the light that is within you, in order to maintain forever a light that has never before existed, until now.

Beloved Friends! Yes, you live in a truly special time. That is why we remind you more and more often to first live your light, and then your energy. We see how strongly all your old images and concepts resist this within you. Be comforted, as we are always with you. Our communications will become something completely natural to you, if you would like them to.

We love you the way you are, the way you act, think, and feel, as in everything there exists the Love that connects us. We love you—within the lightness of Love!

    Your Star Children

God — Multiplicity

A very good morning to you, you pure Child of Man! It is so nice to sit across from you in your beauty. Our message for today is meant to remind you how easily you can find God. It is not the first time that you sit there and wait for God. You have already done this countless times, and every time you noticed that God is here and was waiting for you. God receives you with His Love. We love you, our bright, radiant star. It is you who takes part in this adventurous game, again and again. "What game?" you will probably ask now. The game of holding something else in the midst of your life to be true beyond merely yourself in human form. God is often a refuge for you. The closer you feel to God, the more God means to you. Sometimes, then, God even means EVERYTHING to you. Isn't it good to realize that God is everything?

God is depicted in your world in so many ways. Kindly, loving, nurturing, creating, and even destroying. Others do not want to depict God at all. They prefer not to make an image of God for themselves. Every idea, every idealized image of God, and also every anti-image, is at least a search for God. In truth God is EVERYTHING. You human beings have admitted the validity of this concept only to a limited extent, as otherwise God would be everywhere and everyone, your friend and also your foe. You don't want that, do you? Well, we say to you: if you open your eyes, then everything you see is God. If you close your eyes, then everything that you don't see is God. Even if you close your eyes, you see God. In everything that you gaze upon you perceive the power of creation. Yes, it is up to you how you interpret this creative energy and whether you consider it to be something good or bad. If something reveals itself to you in Love, it is easy to recognize God within it. But how is it possible to also recognize God in all of everything else, since we have just said that God is in everything?

Your assessment of "godliness" takes place from a certain point of view. This point of view is the justification and guarantee of one's own position and of one's own life. Think about it for a minute—everyone sees God from this standpoint! And everyone can recognize God, as this ability is in all of you. Can you in this way better understand that God is everything? From your point of view, God is only that wherein you want to see God, for the time being, until you can recognize God in everything and God becomes everything. And this perception exists just as often on the Earth as there are people on it as well. To put it another way, you see and recognize God in that which you love. But there is something else, which you fear and reject. And now, consider the standpoint of another person. Perhaps he shows himself at that moment in an aspect that you easily reject, and that he himself loves—he sees God in it? Don't all the human ways of seeing things turn everything into God, in the way that they compliment and complete one another? Thus God doesn't have to be merely that which you love anymore! This realization contains for human reason, which primarily orientates itself to polarity, the opportunity to consider the Divine Presence in everything to be at least possible, except if you say that your perception of things is more accurate, better, and more valid than that of other people. Then you allow only your image of God to hold sway. What do you think now? Is God in everything? In everything within which people wish to see the Divine? And every person wants to recognize the Divine in other, different aspects of things. Isn't that a great system? Doesn't God manifest Himself already by means of every one of these human perceptions in your consciousness? Is that perhaps Divine Love?

We love you, valued Child of Man! Through your perception you realize that God makes a community and a common ground possible within the secular multiplicity. All of you come from Divine Consciousness. There is nothing wrong with you, dear human being! All of your human longing for something greater shows that you are on the path. Much of what you have achieved is proof that you as a human being have felt abandoned and in this belief had to do something to replenish this emptiness. Love and the recognition of God in everything satisfied your hunger for vindication. It will help to relieve your oscillation between the human and the divine consciousness, until you no longer see a contradiction between divine and human actions. Then you will have actualized God in everything. If you deal gently with your human perception of things, then you can turn them into Divine Perception!

Everything that you love, you turn into Love—this is alchemy.

Your Divine Consciousness expands your earthly consciousness. So open your side blinders! Your life will become wide, loving, powerful, and lively, as everything in which you sense life to be, you awaken to life.

Do you see in all this the wonderful tactics of God? God gives every human being the possibility to recognize Him. You recognize your human perception by the fact that it only wants to see God in that by means of which it justifies itself. Your balancing act in life consists of allowing divine and human perception to become one. Now you can swing back and forth with joy and ease between your human and your divine perception, until they are then one, until you turn them into a single point of view. The only thing it takes is remembering your Divine Consciousness. For that reason we keep on calling you, and are happy whenever you hear us.

There is so much Love in all of you—you need it on the Earth. What is preventing you from using it, from living it out? In that way you make God manifest at that point on the Earth where you find yourself, as in Heaven you don't need to make God a reality!

We thank you, our beloved friend, that you have obeyed our Love. Your openness refreshes your life again and again. You are beautiful the way you are. We all love you. You achieve such wonderful things in your life. You allow your Divine Consciousness to grow in such a courageous way. Love and joy are yours. The power is yours. Can you see this? Or do you think that God favors all of those who want to be model pupils and teacher's pets?

Everything is Love—in radiant joy! Shine on!

Your Friends and Beloveds, who love you more than anything else.

    The Star Children

Treasure Chest

You are very welcome, you courageous, wonderful person, who always seeks us! I am the inner voice of Love. I am soft as velvet—I am demanding. That sounds unusual to you, doesn't it? Yes, I am demanding! What do I demand? Demanding means demanding—and thus I am demanding! What do I demand? Love! Love is absolutely essential to your life. Love demands a little willingness from you. That is what Love demands and demands, willingness to get involved with me—with the inner voice of Love.

......

We greet you, our dear, patient earthly pilgrim! We tell you today how courted, accompanied, and loved you are. You are afraid that today we will speak to you for the last time? Beloved, you know that we are always with you. You ask if you should pass on our message of Love to others? Yes, that is a great joy, as in that way you have become one—that is the really good aspect of it! You have understood that it is you who come into contact with us with the vibration of Love. Our entire Love, our being, exists independently from your time and your space. Thus it is you who always enters into our time and our space.

God thought you up. God conceived you, in Love. Yes, you are a creature made from Love. Now you will perhaps ask how you can live out this Love in your daily life. We wish to motivate you to do so, as bringing yourself closer to Love, that is, your true being, is an act of creation that you are capable of. Allowing yourself as a person to live out your spiritual connection is an act of creation that you are capable of.

As you know, we always love you. Your goal should be to discover your creative abilities as a human being. You came here to the Earth in order to experience that everything that God can do, you can do as well. The Love that God is "capable of"—you are capable of it, too! The only thing you can really obtain in this life is Love—as Love is creative energy and true consciousness. Love is the All-Embracing Source. One side of Divine Love is human love. The goal, all longing, of human Love is the center, the Oneness.

Another expression of Divine Love is your deeds. They are the reflection of your degree of consciousness. Your human desire should melt into your deepest inner desires!

It is your Love that changes the world.

You do know how many people are waiting for the Love of other human beings or the Spiritual World. All right, who should start to bring this love to awareness? Always the others? This is your opportunity to transform yourself into God. Love is energy. Love is peace. Love is joy. Love is everything. If Love is everything then you are also Love! Is this enough motivation for you to feel this joy?

Beloved Earthling! We are accompanying you throughout your earthly journey until you know that your entire being is conceived in Love. We know how easy it is to wish for pain and punishment for yourself, as you are used to it. We value the challenge that you humans have taken on in earthly life: to lift everything into the consciousness of Love. Now you will probably ask how that is supposed to happen? We know the moments in which you have already been at one with yourself, with creation, with Love in your life. It often happened without you having reckoned with it! So, it is possible!

We want to tell you now that we are at your side at all times. We are always at your side as helpers and counselors, whenever you need us, whenever you have forgotten who you truly are.

Your Being is Divine Being!

We love you with our whole hearts and wish you for your journey through life, through the various dimensions, that you live out your true potential of Love! It is a great joy for us to see your growth, your hope, your confidence! Just imagine: every human being carries this potential within himself! Hasn't God taken good care of the world? Everything that you need is within you. Make use of the Divine Treasure Chest! Your trip as a commuter through the various dimensions of consciousness is a true act of bravado! Everything that you wish for on these planes is reality!

We love you—we love you—we love you!
OM Elohim
In solidarity—in freedom—in Love!

    Your Star Children

Appeal

Beloved Brothers and Sisters in the heart of the One who gives life to us all. This is an appeal.

Yes, this is the first time that we greet you in this way. An appeal, what can that mean? You surely think now that it has to do with an appeal for Love. For what else would your friends from the stars make an appeal, anyway? And an appeal even sounds a little like a kind of missionary activity, into the bargain, doesn't it? We appeal to you to finally esteem a part of you that is becoming more and more important in this special time on Earth and in universal time: it is your divine nature. Particularly now, there is to be found among you human Souls an interesting striving for your true nature. You are asking yourselves where you come from, who you are, and where you are going. And of course you have your tasks HERE on the Earth. Yes, we speak of tasks! You were given tasks. Nevertheless we say to you and to all of you that it is now time to turn your attention to your Divine Task!

What is your Divine Task? It is firstly and most importantly to recognize that your life was provided with a Love that is unimaginable to you. That is, so much trust has been placed in you in regard to your earthly service that you could never comprehend it by means of your earthly thought alone. The trust of which we are speaking here has nothing to do with human trust, as this resembles more a business term in an economic context. As human beings you always trust just that far as is useful to your momentary standpoint. This sounds more oriented towards business practices, doesn't it? No, Beloved! The trust that has been placed in you at your arrival on the Earth and that always accompanies you is a Divine Trust, unconditional trust! You came to the Earth with Love and trust as well as an irrefutable certainty and strength, as all this is needed here. All this corresponds to your nature.

Look at it from this angle: **you incarnated on the Earth in this time of change of consciousness so that you might live out all these qualities, instead of having to learn them!** Yes, that corresponds to your divine nature. You are guided in the deepest way by this Love and energy. This is your true motivation. All of this has nothing to do with escapism—quite the opposite. Your divine nature manifests itself now on the Earth. It is now incumbent on all of you to recognize your divinity and the divinity in everything, or divinity as such, here on the Earth. By recognizing this you make it manifest, and that is what our appeal is all about.

Don't put up anymore with being more affected by negativity than from the positive, divine radiance. As a human being you form your life by means of your consciousness and your knowledge. This life is no detached or isolated affair. You see that all human lives are working on the consciousness of the Earth at the same time! That is a divine act. And the ability to see the balance once again in everything, or the balance and the divine creativity in everything, springs from your **Divine Nature**. As a result of your earthly experiences and memories you have grown accustomed to concentrating on stagnated and human aspects. The core of your being has nothing to do with stagnation, however. Setting your ineffable Love, your indescribable light free on the earth cannot be held back! For all of you who feel the impressive developments in your times: it is of global and universal importance that you fulfill this other part, this divine part in you!!! The wonderful thing is that it is quite easy if you look at it from your divine standpoint. This is our call and our appeal to you.

It has nothing to do with wanting to appear better, greater, or superior. The greatest thing that you can accept is your divinity. It is not even a meter away from you.

> **Instead of saying divinity is within you all, it is more accurate to say that you exist within divinity.**

This is by far the greater part of you. This is your mission. For everything that you do or do not do on the Earth, the entire Divine Power stands behind you. And we say now for that reason "behind you," because you can take this more easily into your human reasoning.

Beloved Friends in the service of Mankind! Our Love caresses you constantly. You can allow yourselves to fall into it. It is your radiant core. It starts with you and reflects the cosmic Love and energy.

We love you, we love you all! We serve everyone.
Your friends that love you so ineffably!

The Star Children

Portrait of the Author

Wolfgang Racher—Ishvara Elohim was born in 1970 in Austria, grew up in the vicinity of the "Salzkammergut" area in Upper Austria, and lives in Vienna.

Even in childhood those in his immediate surroundings became aware of his mediumistic and healing talents. Obeying his inner voice, he was soon drawn to healers, shamans, and spiritual masters on other continents. He broadened his knowledge of healing in multiple dimensions of consciousness.

With the help of his spiritual connections, the author was guided through a childhood full of illness and other challenges. Since his younger days he has given mediumistic expression to a broad spectrum of mental energies which support the Earth and its creatures as a helper in this "time of upheaval."

His great love of music found expression in the study of music in Vienna and in training as a conductor. For the author, sound is not only one of the many means of communicating within the various levels of consciousness, but is also a carrier of creative energy.

Ishvara Elohim is able to bring people in all situations in life closer to Love as the meaning of life by means of a consciousness that has nothing to do with escapism. In his energy work he is very careful to differentiate between the various energies that can compromise a person's health and his happiness. In order to bring physical and emotional symptoms into balance effectively, he advises handing over healing to the highest spiritual level of creativity as an act of consciousness.

As a critical observer of "mainstream esotericism" the author regards the flight of many people to spirituality as a symptom of resignation in the face of the present day. The message of his book, *The Star Children-Elohim*, is an invitation to every reader to accept the beauty of one's own Soul in the here and now, instead of becoming dependent on the illusion of waiting for better times…

To contact the author: freispruch@outlook.com

www.ingramcontent.com/pod-product-compliance
Lightning Source LLC
LaVergne TN
LVHW020932090426
835512LV00020B/3316